GLOBETROTTER™

Travel Guide

WITHDRAWN

SEYCHELLES

Paul Tingay

NEW
HOLLAND

D1234062

NEW
HOLLAND

Sixth edition published in 2015
by MapStudio™
10 9 8 7 6 5 4 3 2 1
www.globetrottertravelguides.com

Distributed in Africa by
MapStudio™
Unit 3, Block B, M5 Park, Eastman Road,
Maitland 7405, Cape Town, South Africa
PO Box 193, Maitland 7404

Distributed in the UK/Europe/Asia by
John Beaufoy Publishing Ltd

Distributed in the USA by
National Book Network

ISBN (Print) 978 1 77026 683 4
ISBN (ePub) 978 1 77026 714 5
ISBN (ePdf) 978 1 77026 715 2

Commissioning Editor: Elaine Fick
DTP Cartographic Manager: Genené Hart
Editors: Elaine Fick, Thea Grobbelaar, Lorissa Bouwer, Mary
Duncan, Donald Reid
Design and DTP: Nicole Bannister, Lyndall Hamilton
Cartographers: Tracey-Lee Fredericks, Reneé Spocter,
Inga Ndibongo, Nicole Bannister
Picture Researcher: Shavonne Govender

Reproduction by Hirt & Carter (Pty) Ltd, Cape Town
Printed and bound by Craft Print International Ltd, Singapore

Acknowlegdements:
The publishers and author would like to thank Alan Mason,
André Rassool, Mifa Monthy, Mia Dunford and Nadine
Etienne, all of Seychelles, and the most helpful staff of the
Seychelles Tourism Board.

Photographic credits:
Anthony Bannister, page 81; Camerapix, page 49; Martin
Harvey, pages 13, 102, 111, 116, 118, 119, 120, 121; Images
of Africa (IOA), page 34; Stefania Lamberti, pages 83, 112,
115; Buddy Mays, pages 92, 114; Fiona McIntosh/IOA, pages
50, 72; Ian Michler, page 9; Gilbert J Pool (courtesy Paul
Tingay), pages 16, 45; Alain Proust, page 32; South African
Library, page 22; Paul Tingay, title page, pages 4, 6, 8, 10,
11, 12, 14, 17, 18, 19, 20, 21, 23, 25, 26, 27, 28, 29, 30, 31,
33, 35, 36, 38, 39, 41, 42, 43, 47, 48, 51, 53, 56, 59, 60, 61,
62, 63, 64, 65, 66, 67, 68, 69, 75, 76, 77, 78, 79, 82, 84, 85,
86, 88, 95, 96, 97, 98, 99, 105, 106, 107, 109, 110, 113, 122;
Travel Pictures Ltd, cover.

Keep us current
Information in travel guides is apt to change, which is why
we regularly update our guides. We'd be grateful to receive
feedback if you've noted something we should include in
our updates. If you have new information, please share
it with us by writing to the Commissioning Editor at the
MapStudio address on this page. The most significant
contribution to each new edition will receive a free copy of
the updated guide.

Front Cover: *Fisherman's Cove, Bel Ombre,
Mahé Island.*
Title Page: *L'Archipel, Côte d'Or, Praslin Island.*

CONTENTS

1
Introducing Seychelles

Emeralds in a forgotten sea, islands of love, a garden of Eden. The soaring mountains of Seychelles, covered with lush jungle, emerge from deep blue seas and a hundred glistening reefs. These Indian Ocean islands, numbering 115 in all, stretch in a jewelled crescent from the equator to the tip of Madagascar. With a population of just over 90,000 Kreol-speaking inhabitants, whose ancestors came from Africa, Arabia, India, Europe, Persia and even China, Seychelles was unknown until the airport sprung the Aladdin's Cave of tourism.

Many of the islands are tiny palm-tufted coral specks where yours may be the only yacht to weigh anchor in a year. **Aldabra**, the world's largest raised atoll and a World Heritage Site, is home to 150,000 giant tortoises. In the high mist forests of **Mahé** and **Silhouette** there are bats that eat mangoes, pitcher plants that gobble insects, and pygmy piping frogs the size of an emerald. The extraordinary beauty of the islands is such that nearly half of Seychelles' land-mass has been set aside as national park.

Mahé is a Bali Hai of scimitar beaches, jungle mountains and secluded coves. 'Once you've seen the damn place,' one exhausted seaman wrote, 'you'll never want to leave.' Tales of pirate treasure abound, plantation houses fade away under breadfruit trees and on **Praslin** unique and erotic male and female coco de mer palms reach to heaven. Catamaran fast-boats call at **La Digue**, where oxcarts trundle along the roads. Some islands are strictly for the birds, others have a solitary lodge, many, a mirage across the ocean.

TOP ATTRACTIONS

*** **Beau Vallon Beach, Mahé:** a classic sweep of sand, waves, and chunky takamaka trees.
*** **Morne Seychellois National Park:** a mountainous living museum of exotic birds and plants.
** **Vallée de Mai, Praslin:** the home of the unique coco de mer forest.
** **Ste Anne Marine National Park:** exquisite fish and corals close to Mahé.
** **Denis Island:** sea birds, lush forest, aquamarine seas.
* **La Digue:** take the Cat Rose catamaran ferry service from Praslin to the most traditional of the main islands.

◄ *Opposite: Palms, surf and hidden coves.*

INTRODUCING SEYCHELLES

THE LAND

Millions of years ago as fires burned and melted in the bowels of the earth, the supercontinent of Gondwana, which included much of the southern hemisphere, tore itself apart. India separated from Africa, the sea rushed in to fill gaping canyons, and deserts and plains were covered by fathomless ocean. It was a process that spanned aeons and embraced the genesis of countless new species of life on earth. Gradually the seasons settled to a gentler rhythm, and the continents assumed their familiar shapes. Left in the middle of the Indian Ocean after this awesome cataclysm were the tips of some of the highest mountains and a hundred isolated coral atolls, a necklace of pearls in a forgotten sea, islands that we now know as Seychelles.

The Granitic Islands

Scattered across some 450,000km² (174,000 sq miles) of sea in the western Indian Ocean, the islands of Seychelles are made up of two distinct geological types: coralline and granitic. Most mid-oceanic islands in the world are formed from coral and volcanic action; the exceptions are the Inner Islands of the Seychelles, which are the remnants of continental Gondwanaland.

Mahé, the largest island, together with **Praslin, La Digue, Silhouette** and the other granitic islands closest to them, account for nearly 50% of the Seychelles' landmass. These are the islands where most Seychellois live, and where the majority of visitor facilities are located. They are all situated in a tight group in the northeastern part of the archipelago, 1600km (1000 miles) from Africa. Apart from towering black granite cliffs high in the mountains and the sensuous, sculptured

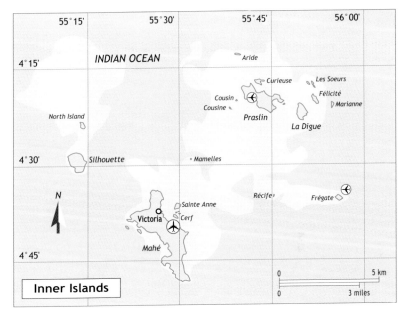

55°15' 55°30' 55°45' 56°00'

4°15' INDIAN OCEAN Aride

Curieuse Les Soeurs
Cousin Félicité
Cousine Marianne
Praslin
La Digue

North Island

4°30' Silhouette Mamelles

N

Récife Frégate

Sainte Anne
Victoria Cerf

Mahé

4°45'

Inner Islands

0 5 km
0 3 miles

boulders that frame many deserted beaches, the granitic islands give the impression of being covered in impenetrable jungle. Mahé's mountainous Morne Seychellois National Park is a wilderness of tangled tropical splendour, but much of the greenery also comes from the profusion of coconut palms, wild cinnamon, and graceful *albizia* trees.

Mahé's beaches and coves are a continuous delight. They all have palms and gnarled *takamaka* trees shading them, the water is crystal clear and the swimming safer than most countries. A few hundred metres in front of most beaches are long lines of rumbling white water at the edge of the reef. The coastline is dotted with airy bungalows, each village with its own church bell tower, crowded general store and small guesthouses.

Some 40km (25 miles) east of Mahé and constantly visible as a blue ridge on the horizon, the second-largest island, Praslin, hides the fabled coco de mer palm in its forested hills. La Digue, near Praslin, has one village, one

◀ *Opposite: A cascade of granite 500 million years old.*

NATIONAL SYMBOLS

• The Seychelles coat of arms displays two sailfish and a tropicbird around a crest which includes a tortoise, a coco de mer, a schooner, and a green island.
• The national flower is the tropicbird orchid.
• The national bird is the Seychelles black parrot (it's actually brown), the only parrot on the islands.
• Air Seychelles, partnered with Etihad Airways, features a new logo of fairy terns courting.

▲ *Above: An aerial view of Bird Island.*

LIVING CORAL

All the coral islands of Seychelles were created from millions of skeletons of tiny animals called polyps.

• Living polyps on the surface of the coral are attached to the limestone base of skeletons beneath them.

• At meal times the polyps capture tiny plankton particles by swishing their sticky tentacles in the sea.

• El Niño's warm current killed many corals, but they are now recovering.

• Soft corals, leather corals and fan corals are the most beautiful. Other types are brain, stag and antler.

• The collecting of coral in Seychelles is not allowed, but there are plenty of attractive (dead) pieces on the beaches.

supermarket, and unique pink-tinged granite boulders among an abundance of palms and delightful little coves. Silhouette, the third-largest island, is to most people a mist-shrouded peak visible from Mahé's Beau Vallon Beach. Other smaller granitic islands (some are resorts) are dispersed around the larger ones, a number of them bird and nature sanctuaries.

The Coralline Islands

The 74 coral islands and atolls of Seychelles are the far-flung outposts of the group. They make up 47% of the land area of the Seychelles, yet only a thousand of the islands' population of 90,000 live on them. During the last Ice Age the level of the Indian Ocean was much lower and there were thousands more, including now-submerged fishing banks.

Denis Island and **Bird Island**, both coral islands, are normally grouped with the Inner Islands. The rest – tiny, horizon-floating islands tufted with palms – are collectively called the Outer Islands, or *zil elwayen* in Kreol, and are spread out like diamond dust across a vast expanse of ocean.

Many of them are only 3m (10ft) above sea level. Some islands have remote lagoons; all have windswept palms, talcum beaches and magical underwater gardens. **Aldabra** and **Farquhar**, the furthest from Mahé, each have a dozen islands, and the **Amirantes** group, named after the Portuguese explorer Admiral Vasco da Gama, twice that. Aldabra atoll, a ring of ferociously pitted limestone coral enclosing a lagoon 34km (21 miles) across, is a World Heritage Site and home to 150,000 giant tortoises, 2000 breeding turtles, and huge, tree-climbing crabs.

Ocean and Reef

The Indian Ocean dominates the Seychelles, whether by the immense depth of water just beyond the reefs, the influence of the oceanic weather patterns, or simply in the vast distances between the little specks of islands. Most visitors will come into contact with the ocean in some form or another: swimming in the warm, protected waters, or sailing on a yacht between the islands. Where meeting the ocean really becomes special, however, is underwater, diving and snorkelling on the edges of a vast new world of coral, waving polyps, fish, and overwhelming silence.

▲ *Above: Go down to the sea and marvel at the wonders of the deep. Goggling with flippers and snorkel is a delight in Seychelles.*

After millions of years, even the granite islands have an encompassing ring of bright corals. Albeit under threat from marinas development. Coral atolls and islands are normally the result of coral growing around a geological formation, such as a volcano, which has sunk into the sea, leaving the crust of coral in place. Coral is a living force, always growing, changing, and offering life to a vast chain of sea creatures, from minute plankton to a myriad flashing fish, porpoises and whales that find the waters of Seychelles so attractive.

Off some shores in the islands the reef is close to the shore and exposed at low tide, which makes for fascinating exploration, while along the beaches themselves you will always be able to find the scattered, delicate artistry of shells and dead coral.

SEYCHELLES	J	F	M	A	M	J	J	A	S	O	N	D
MAX TEMP. ºC	30	30	31	32	31	28	29	29	29	30	30	30
MIN TEMP. ºC	25	25	26	26	26	25	24	25	25	25	25	25
MAX TEMP. ºF	86	86	88	90	88	82	84	84	84	86	86	86
MIN TEMP. ºF	77	77	79	79	79	77	75	77	77	77	77	77
RAINFALL mm	541	177	249	168	81	158	52	93	300	246	217	335
RAINFALL in	21	7	10	7	3	6	2	4	12	10	9	13
DAYS OF RAINFALL	12	15	15	14	14	12	12	11	12	13	17	19

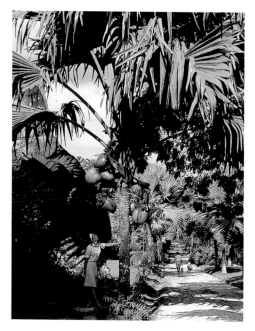

▲ *Above: A young female coco de mer tree.*

LULU THE GHOST CRAB

Trouloulou, in Kreol, the ghost crab, is the mischievous thief of the sands. It preys on hatchling turtles and is in turn preyed upon by fishermen who use these delicate sand dancers as bait. Lulu is hilarious to watch, particularly at night, peak revelry time, as she skitters in jerkstart six-by-six sprints across a pristine moonlit beach. Frightened, she will hunker down pretending to be invisible, then rush on tiny tiptoes for burrow or surf.

Climate

Seychelles lies in the tropics between 4° and 10°S of the equator. The average daily **temperature** is 29°C (84°F), the average **humidity** a steamy 80% and there are about seven hours of **sunshine** daily. The refreshing *ven di swet* **trade winds** blow from April to October, when the weather tends to be cooler and drier, while the lighter northwest monsoon winds arrive during the Christmas period. At this time the **rain** can fall in torrential downpours, but there are short, showery spells any time of year. The force of the tropical showers means that the annual rainfall is around 2500mm (99in), which is nearly four times that of London. However, being small islands in a wide ocean, Seychelles' many microclimates ensure conditions are very localized — it can be raining on one beach, sunny on the next and misty up in the mountains.

The islands are at their windiest from April to September, which are the best sailing months. The coral islands are drier, warmer and, being at sea level, usually catch refreshing sea breezes. Only Farquhar atoll is within the storm winds cyclone belt.

Plant Life

The shoreline of the main granitic islands was once a jungle of almost impenetrable 30m (100ft) tall hardwood trees, but settlement, naval rivalry during the Napoleonic wars and plantations soon devastated those. Even today, however, the impression is still of a botanic riot of dense breadfruit trees, flame trees, banyans and bananas, and everywhere an unwelcome creeper called Lalayann d'Argent or elephant climber. Old coconut and cinnamon plantations are everywhere, and wild fruits grow in every back yard: mangoes, bananas, tamarinds, star-shaped *karambol*, fluffy fruited *prunes de France*, and prickly *frisiter*. Alongside the requisite ubiquitous palms on every beach, there are shading *takamaka* and casuarina trees, whose tiny cones create a minefield for barefoot bathers. Among the 103 tree and plant species unique to Seychelles are the wild *bilenbi*, whose tart fruit actually grows on the trunk of the tree, and possibly the rarest tree on earth, the *bwa mediz* or jellyfish tree. Lost to botanists since 1908, its rediscovery 60 years later caused quite a stir at Kew Gardens in London. There are only about 50 in the world, all in the high mountains of Mahé. It is a bushy, rather unspectacular tree, which takes its name, jellyfish, from its umbrella-shaped fruit. A total of 1108 species of plants grow in Seychelles of which 69 are endemic, while 257 species (34 endemic) flourish mainly in the coralline islands. Shore plants include casuarinas, coconuts and hardy mangroves.

Lording over the botanical castle, however, is the giant **coco de mer palm**, whose male catkins and double female nuts bear a striking resemblance to the respective human reproductive organs. The Vallée de Mai nature reserve on Praslin Island is the largest natural preserve of these monster palms which are endemic to (i.e. they originate uniquely from) Seychelles.

Creatures of Land, Sea and Air

Seychelles may once have been linked to Africa and India but it has no big game. The only endemic mammal in residence is the giant fruit bat. This flying fox boasts a 1m wingspan, and unlike other bats, can see.

Giant land tortoises are only found in two places in the world: the Galapagos islands off South America, and Seychelles. They grow up to half a metre (1.6ft) high, weigh 150kg (330lb) and at least some are

▼ Below: Blue-black beak and mischievous eyes characterize the Seychelles fairy tern.

INTRODUCING SEYCHELLES

believed to be 200 years old. The ancient Greeks thought tortoises, *tartaroukhos*, came from the underworld; hence their name. There are five types of frogs in the islands, croaking in competitive concert in the mountains. The female tree frog grows up to 20cm (8in), somewhat over-shadowing her spouse, who measures a mere 5cm (2in). After the early extermination of the Nile crocodiles, the only other land reptiles are geckos, skinks and a large endemic chameleon. The bright emerald green gecko will shed its wriggling tail as a ruse to distract an advancing predator.

There are 3500 insect species in Seychelles, most unique to the islands, including Frégate Island's giant tenebrionid beetle, and the Seychelles leaf insect, whose camouflage drag far outclasses the African variety. There are surprisingly few butterflies in Seychelles other than on the islands of the Aldabra group.

Millions of birds migrate from as far as the Arctic Circle to the coral islands of Seychelles to breed. Some of the islands, such as Aride and Cousine, host some spectacular and noisy colonies of sea birds, including noddies, terns and frigate birds. A number of land varieties are unique to Seychelles, and are constantly under threat of extinction. Amongst these are the Magpie Robin, Seychelles kestrel, blue pigeon, bulbul, the beautiful black paradise flycatcher, and the whistling black parrot of the coco de mer palms on Praslin.

▶ *Right: A giant tortoise, often confused with and closely related to the turtle.*
▶▶ *Opposite: Both animals are found in Seychelles. The turtle has a flatter shell, and its legs have developed into paddle-like flippers.*

Sea Life

Dolphins, whales and manta rays are all common in Seychelles waters. The dugong or sea cow was once here too and is remembered in the original name for Bird Island, Île aux Vaches (Isle of Cows). The larger sharks usually stay in deep waters, although the plankton-feeding whale shark, the largest fish in the world, is sometimes encountered by divers. The marine

turtle nests on a number of the islands, though nowadays all four species in Seychelles – green, hawksbill, loggerhead, and the giant leatherback – are continuously hunted by that relentless predator, man, and are carefully monitored and protected. Fighting fish such as marlin and under-threat tuna are caught in the waters around the islands. The most beautiful is the sailfish, which will leap out of the water shivering its silvery blue body in the sun.

Along the coral reefs there are a thousand flashing, darting and amazingly colourful reef fish. In the underwater forest you will see angelfish, parrotfish, cave-defending moray eels, hovering trumpetfish and the occasional turtle winging away in fright. There are black spiky urchins, tiger cowries, half-metre long crayfish and, occasionally, the protected *triton* conch shell blown by fishermen in early days to announce fish for sale.

Conserve with Care

Although 46% of Seychelles land area is protected in one form or another, it often seems as if the whole of Seychelles is one large and extraordinarily beautiful park: island and beach, mountain and forest, reef and ocean.

The 18ha (45-acre) **Vallée de Mai** on Praslin, the home of the coco de mer palms, is one of Seychelles' two World Heritage Sites. The other is the 34km (21-mile) long **Aldabra** atoll, with its giant tortoises, rare birds and green turtle

DEVIL OF THE DEEP

The plankton-eating manta ray, or *diable de mer*, does not deserve its demonic name, for you cannot find a more graceful and harmless creature in the warm tropical waters. They look like stealth bombers, their pectoral wings spanning up to 7m (23ft), often in flights of six or more. They can weigh as much as 1300kg (2900lb). Seychelles fishermen used to harpoon them from small craft, but the manta is powerful and will easily drag a boat. The devil-fish tag comes from the hornlike fins on either side of its head. In the days of slavery, plantation owners were fond of whips made from manta tail.

INTRODUCING SEYCHELLES

TURTLE SANCTUARY

Not long ago turtles from the outer islands would be stacked like boxes on the decks of ships, and, crying and sighing all the while, transported to the Long Pier pool on Mahé to be slaughtered for steaks, salted *kitouz*, and the *calipee* (fat) used in Europe to make turtle soup. Their yellow ping-pong-ball eggs were also stolen to make cakes. They have survived for over 100 million years yet now are threatened with extinction. In times past 6000 green turtles were caught annually in Cosmoledo. Today in neighbouring Aldabra breeding females are steadily expanding. Harpooning turtles and (horrors!) flipping over egg-laying mothers on the beach at night will land you in jail. Christmas is a blessed time on Denis and other islands when the gentle creatures produce their teensy flippering hatchlings.

breeding grounds. Tiny **Cousin Island** is administered by Nature Seychelles, while its sibling **Cousine** is a privately funded nature conservancy. Not too far away on La Digue Island the small **La Veuve Reserve** has successfully doubled the number of endangered long-tailed Seychelles Black Paradise Flycatchers from 300 to 600, with some translocated to Denis Island. Others are nurtured and protected on Curieuse Island.

Sea birds may not be disturbed on nine designated islands and spear fishing is prohibited everywhere. 'Live' shells may not be collected or taken home in your luggage. Ironically they sell openly (see Antoine Manes' beautiful collection, Fiennes Esplanade, Victoria). On some of the islands where the tree populations were devastated by plantations, reforestation and bird relocation schemes have been introduced. The ceiling placed on the number of hotel beds by government some time ago is today subject to continuous pressure from foreign investors and government's perceived need to generate forex. This could gradually gnaw at the island's unique and fragile ecosystem.

HISTORY IN BRIEF

The Indian Ocean is the birthplace of long-distance sailing. Ancient Indian, Egyptian and Chinese texts, even DNA, indicate that there was sea-borne trade between India, China and Africa as long ago as 2000BCE (Before Common Era) possibly involving the traders of Crete's Atlantis as well. Polynesians setting out from the Bay of Bengal on their great canoes sailed east into the Pacific, and Indonesians west to the Maldives and Madagascar. The Phoenicians are known

▼ *Below: A pirogue fisherman where nowadays jets come in to land.*

to have rounded the southern tip of Africa and Indian sailors commissioned by the kings of Gujerat in the 6th century were colonizing Java, Bali and Madagascar. It is more than likely that some of these intrepid sailors stumbled upon the tiny mid-oceanic islands of the Seychelles on their voyages, possibly taking a little time to explore them, catch a turtle that offered some longed-for fresh meat, and perhaps plant a few crops to sustain them, before disappearing on their way again over the blue horizon.

Dhows in the Sea of Zanj

The first written record of the Seychelles (there may be Chinese texts and Cretan artefacts still submerged) dates from CE851, a time when Arab merchant seamen from the Persian Gulf in their lateen-rigged dhows made good use of the January winds blowing from India towards Africa, and then the opposite southeast monsoon a few months later, to navigate the ocean they called the Sea of Zanj, or Sea of Blacks.

In CE916, the geographer Abu Zaid al Hassan referred to the 'high islands beyond the Maldives', which is generally considered to be a reference to the uniquely mountainous Seychelles. The Arabs called the granitic Inner Islands of the Seychelles 'Zarin', or Sisters – a possible reference to the seven sisters of the Pleiades constellation – and as they are known to have brought the first coconut palm from India to the East African coast they may well have introduced it to Seychelles too. It is also clear that the coco de mer (which is endemic to Seychelles) was valued by Indian and Maldivan princes. At Anse Lascars on Silhouette and on Frégate Island there are Arab graves and ruins of coral brick buildings.

Chinese and Portuguese Pioneers

Five hundred years ago, soon after a huge Chinese fleet had abandoned the Indian Ocean for good, tiny Portuguese caravels under the command of **Vasco da Gama** braved storms and scurvy to journey around the Cape of Good Hope towards India and Japan. The Amirantes Islands of the

THE ROC

Arab sailors believed the Seychelles to be the islands of the mythological *rukh*, or giant roc bird. The legends said that the coco de mer tree grew up from beneath the ocean (hence its name – coco de mer, or coconut of the sea), and its branches provided a roosting place for the mighty bird with its 45m (150ft) wingspan which could carry off elephants, and would surely do the same to any sailor who came too close. Marco Polo recounted this tale to Kublai Khan in China 700 years ago, who immediately dispatched an envoy with instructions to return with a quill from the fabulous bird.

INTRODUCING SEYCHELLES

Seychelles, or the 'Isles of the Admiral', were named in 1502 in honour of Da Gama's promotion to the rank, but these first Europeans were not destined to settle on any of the islands they encountered. Within a few years the Portuguese had destroyed the Arab trade stranglehold on the Indian Ocean, and Portuguese names now dot the ocean map: Chagos, Comoros, Rodrigues, Agalega, Diego Garcia and Cosmoledo, the latter atoll a part of Seychelles.

Surveys, Spices, and Settlements

The first Englishmen to visit the islands that were to become their colony did so in 1609, with diarist **John Jourdain** giving us the first detailed picture of Seychelles. A hundred years later English and American pirates, harried out of the Caribbean, turned their swashbuckling attentions from the Spanish Main to the trade of spices, silks, tea and timber that was crisscrossing the Indian Ocean. Famous buccaneers such as **Captain Kidd, 'Long Ben' Avery, Tom Tew**, and hook-nosed **Olivier le Vasseur** (known as *La Buse*, the Buzzard) roamed the lucrative seas, and found the deserted coves of Seychelles ideal places to hide, careen ships and bury plunder.

A rusty old anchor at Anse Boileau beach on Mahé marks the spot where French Captain **Lazare Picault** landed in 1742 to survey the Seychelles for Governor Mahé de Labourdonnais of Mauritius. He gave the island the name Île d'Abondance, and only later Mahé, in honour of his superior. Fourteen years were to pass before Commander **Corneille Nicholas Morphey** (of Irish-French descent) laid the official Stone of Possession on the shore of Victoria harbour, and –

BOILED TORTOISE, MR MIDSHIPMAN?

The English East Indiaman, the *Ascension*, anchored in Seychelles for 10 days in 1609. John Jourdain, one of the crew, wrote the first known account of the islands:
'About nine in the morninge we descryed heigh land', that had '... noe signe of any people that ever had bene there'. In this 'earthly paradise' they were 'allagartes' and (according to another observer, William Revett) '... many trees of 60 and 70 feete without sprigge except at the topp ... shipp tymber as the lyke or better can-not bee seene'. The crew availed themselves of '... much fishe and fowle and tortells', which the crew, hungry for meat after so long at sea, fell upon, but after a few meals rejected because '... they did looke soe uglie before they were boyled'. Subsequent sailors were to use the heavy tortoises as ballast.

astutely for an aspiring naval officer – renamed the group of islands Séchelles after the French finance minister.

The French authorities in Île-de-France (Mauritius), nervous of British colonial ambitions, were keen to back up their claim with actual occupancy, and so in 1770, encouraged by **Pierre Poivre**, an administrator of Île-de-France who thought Seychelles could rival the Dutch East Indies in the cultivation of spices, the first tiny party of settlers landed on Ste Anne's Island.

A small 'Etablissement du Roi', today's capital, Victoria, was built on Mahé, but the settlers grew few spices, and the colony survived rather than prospered.

Cannonballs and Capitulations

The French Revolution in 1789 set off a series of reactions around Europe that led to 20 years of war and the rise and fall of Napoleon. By 1794, when a new Commandant **Chevalier Jean-Baptiste Queau de Quinssy** arrived in the islands, Britain and France were at war, and the Indian Ocean was of growing strategic importance. The Seychelles were still in theory ruled from Mauritius, but they were remote and vulnerable.

On 16 May 1794, a squally day, when the island had been awake for a mere two hours, Commodore **Henry Newcome** of

THE BUZZARD'S BOOTY

The treasure of buccaneer Olivier le Vasseur is the most famous of the riches supposedly buried around the islands. The search has concentrated around Bel Ombre beach on Mahé, yet neither there, nor on any of the other islands around Seychelles where tantalizing tales of treasure abound, has anything beyond a few silver coins and a pistol or two ever been found. Or if there has, no-one is telling. Still, there is a Pirates Bay, a 'corsair' restaurant, a murdered buccaneer's tombstone in the National Museum, and a Pirates Arms hotel. Roman Polanski filmed *Il Pirato* in Seychelles. And what with a little yo ho ho and a bottle of local Takamaka Bay rum, it all makes sound tourism sense.

◄◄ *Opposite: An old French cannon harkens nostalgically for Napoleonic Empire days.*
◄ *Left: The lure of Seychelles from the time of the first settlers: coconuts, spices, and a marquetry box made from valuable local hardwoods.*

INTRODUCING SEYCHELLES

the British Royal Navy entered Victoria harbour, rather unsportingly flying a French flag. Faced by a combined British squadron firepower of 166 cannon and 12,500 trained men, De Quinssy remonstrated for honour's sake and then surrendered.

Down came the tricolor, up went the Union Jack, to a gentlemanly roll of drums and presentation of arms. Two weeks later the British sailed off, and the tricolor was back at the top of the flagpole with the *au revoirs* still ringing in the air. With alternate visits from French and British men o' war, De Quinssy became rather adept at welcoming first one side, then the other, supplying both with food, water, and a berth for repairs, while all the time acting as a refuge for French corsairs such as the notorious and dashing **Jean François Hodoul**.

Britain captured Mauritus (which still theoretically included the Seychelles) in 1810, but their only concern for the islands was that the enemy did not use them. The mercurial De Quinssy, showing typical political astuteness, anglicized his name to suit his new rulers, became De Quincy, and carried on as Chief Justice on Mahé until his death in 1827.

The Colonial Backwater

At this stage cotton, manioc and a dozen different spices were being grown by a population of 1800, of whom all but

300 were slaves. In 1835 slavery was abolished and Seychelles was obliged to change from field husbandry to a total plantation economy (with crops such as coconuts, cinnamon, vanilla and patchouli) which did not require a large labour force. Former slaves were not interested in working on the plantations

▶ ▶ Opposite: A small farm at Anse Marie-Louise, Praslin, flanks the new Fond Ferdinand coco de mer Heritage reserve.
▶ Right: Jean François Hodoul, renowned gentleman corsair.

where, as they put it, 'the money is good, but too expensive'. The British adopted a policy of landing freed slaves on Seychelles (a total of 2500 over the years) where they were soon hired as labourers under 'apprenticeships', though with stinted rations, inadequate wages and rough treatment, their lives were hardly improved.

Saddled with a poor colony she did not want, Britain allowed Seychelles, for the rest of the 19th century and a good part of the next, to remain a peaceful, rather old-fashioned backwater visited by the occasional steamer and eccentric Victorian traveller. Among these were Marianne North, a botanist painter, and General 'Chinese' Gordon, who developed his quixotic theory of the biblical Genesis among the mysterious coco de mer palms of Praslin Island.

It was during the 19th century of splendid isolation and benign British *laissez faire* that the culture of Seychelles was formed – a mix of master and slave, planter and fisherman, France and Africa. Various crops and industries came and went over the years, including vanilla, copra, cinnamon, guano, and even whaling, but none seemed to last for long. The French farmers disliked their British rulers and in turn the British were disdainful. With the arrival in 1850 of the first Indian merchants and in 1895 a few Chinese, the Kreol kaleidoscope of the islands was complete.

The 20th Century

Seychelles eased gradually into the 20th century. In 1903 she emerged from under the skirts of Mauritius to take up status as a fully fledged colony. To mark this momentous development a Clock Tower was erected in the middle of Victoria, and for over 100 years it has been the centre of

SLAVERY

The first 21 settlers in 1770 on Ste Anne's Island included six slaves, and the economy of the islands was to depend on this cheap labour for the next 70 years. Slavery in the Seychelles was reasonably benevolent and not perhaps as harsh as in other parts of the world, but a person enslaved in the islands still suffered the threat of iron halter, chain and manta ray whip,along with appalling restrictions on movement, possessions, housing, marriage and the right to their children. Worst of all, perhaps, was the memory of abduction and the obliteration of cultural roots. To this day in Seychelles many appear reluctant to marry and the music of the islands, *moutya*, seems at times to reflect an indefinable loss and need for relationship and certainty.

INTRODUCING SEYCHELLES

BORN TO BE KING

In 1805 one Pierre Louis Poiret arrived in Seychelles. He always maintained (as did 40 others) that he was the legitimate heir to the French throne, son of Marie Antoinette and Louis XVI, and that he had been smuggled out of the Temple Prison in Paris and given as a child to a cobbler, whose name, Poiret, he took. Always deferred to with royal respect, he farmed on both Poivre and Mahé Islands and died at the age of 78 in 1858. Although never formally married, he left nine children, all of whom were named, in royal fashion, Louis or Louise.

town and focus of traffic, business and sophistication. In the islands, if you had not seen the *horloge* you were considered a country hick.

During these years, Indian indentured labourers built a road over the mountains to every visitor's favourite beach, Beau Vallon; Catholic churches and two secondary schools were established, and the British administration strived mightily and unsuccessfully to anglicize language and culture. The lovely iron-filigreed hospital near the Botanical Gardens was built: with elephantiasis, amoebic dysentery and leprosy it was much needed. The first car arrived, and in 1926 electricity hesitantly flickered to illuminate the centre of town.

During World War II several contingents of Seychelles soldiers (Pioneer Corps) fought in the desert campaign. For many Seychellois it was the first taste of equality and freedom. Some stayed on in the British army, providing Rs650,000 in wages annually to 3000 poorer families. Their return in the early 1950s was a financial setback, but it was also the source of much excitement. 'Maman, the Tobruks have come back', the folk song went, 'what an occasion, Maman, I'll die or go mad if I don't find a husband.'

Immediately after the war **Dr (Sir) Percy Selwyn-Clarke**, medical officer in the notorious Japanese POW camp at Stanley in Hong Kong, became the first Governor appointed by a socialist government in London. 'I will have no colour bar in this colony', he declared, thus disenfranchising himself immediately in the esteem of the chattering classes down at **The Club**. Victoria's colourful fish and vegetable market is named after him.

A Tale of Two Lawyers

And it was time for politics. A taxpayers' association was formed and in 1940 the

▼ *Below: The Victoria Clock Tower, not long after it was erected to commemorate the granting of full colonial status to Seychelles in 1903.*

◀ *Left: Multicoloured multi-styled buildings match the exotic mix of people and purchases in Market Street Mall, Victoria.*

colonial legislative council permitted four elected members. In 1964, two political parties were formed: the Democratic Party, led by ebullient lawyer **James Mancham** (whose family ran a popular supermarket, Richards', in Victoria), and the broader based Seychelles People's United Party, also led by a lawyer, **Albert René**. For 40 turbulent years these two men remained at the centre of the country's political stage.

Universal adult suffrage arrived in 1967, but the great leap forward for Seychelles was to opt for tourism as the mainstay of the islands' economy. When the airport was constructed in 1971, the landing of the first VC10 was watched by practically the whole island.

Five years later, on 29 June 1976, Seychelles became independent from Britain and the bearded and Saville Row-besuited Mancham took over from the cockaded governor. Henceforth, two portraits adorned public buildings in Seychelles: one of the incumbent, President Mancham, and the other, with a leaner, somewhat hungrier look, of Prime Minister René.

The following year, while James Mancham was at a Commonwealth Conference in London, René pounced with a coup d'état. With Tanzanian troops standing by in Dar es Salaam as a backup, his men took the broadcasting centre, the police station and power. Three men were killed, one –

EXILES IN EDEN

Napoleon banished 80 Jacobin 'terrorists' to Seychelles. The practice was to become established.

• 1876 **Sultan Abdullah of Perak**. His son, Chulan, took back to Malaysia a popular song in Seychelles, *Rosalie*, which under the title *Terang Bulan* (Bright Moon), eventually became that nation's national anthem.

• 1900 **King Prempeh II of Ashanti West Africa**, who arrived dressed in leopard skins, accompanied by his favourite executioner.

• 1916 **Seyyid Khalid bin Barghash of Zanzibar**, sent to Seychelles for being friendly to the Kaiser.

• In 1922 Winston Churchill considered sending 500 **Irish political prisoners** to Praslin.

• 1956 **Archbishop Makarios of Cyprus** stayed a pleasant year, climbed the 905m (2970 ft) Morne Seychellois and reputedly sang well.

• 1981 **Failed coup d'etat** by mercenaries disguised as South African rugby players, 'Ye Ancient Order of Froth-Blowers'. Those caught were later forgiven.

INTRODUCING SEYCHELLES

▲ *Above: James Mancham (right), the country's first president, and Albert René (left), then prime minister, seal an independence deal with Britain in 1976. Both ex-presidents live in Seychelles.*

an insurgent – became a hero while the other – a policeman – did not. Guns appeared in the streets, a curfew was announced, arrests were made and a people's militia formed. The revolution for *liberté, égalité, fraternité* had taken place, but as René was the people's choice anyway, history may well decide that it was unnecessary.

The Modern Era

Changes came quickly in the next two decades. It was, for the Seychellois, the best of times, the worst of times. Tourism soared, the economy boomed, construction flourished. New schools, old-age homes and health facilities all arrived. A confident spirit of nationhood fired *le peuple*, who soon became well nourished, well clothed, educated and employed. But it was also a time of counter-coups, plots and fear. In 1981 a planeload of South African mercenaries, led by 'Mad' Mike Hoare and joined by out-of-work Rhodesian Selous Scouts, launched an abortive invasion masquerading as a rugby team, guns hidden under toys. They were stopped at

HISTORICAL CALENDAR

250 million years ago The supercontinent of Gondwana splits up, leaving a few islands in the Indian Ocean. Among them, Seychelles.

2000BCE – CE500 Chinese, Egyptian, Indian, Greek, Roman and Phoenician explorations of the Indian Ocean. Some probably visit Seychelles.

CE851 First Arab recorded sighting of Seychelles.

1275 Marco Polo tells Kublai Khan of the (mythological) roc bird in the Indian Ocean.

1502 Amirantes islands named

after Admiral Vasco da Gama, Portuguese navigator.

1609 First British landing. Recorded by John Jourdain.

1742 First French landing by Lazare Picault.

1756 Stone of Possession laid on Mahé. Islands named Séchelles; first settlement follows in 1770.

1814 Seychelles ceded to Britain.

1835 Abolition of slavery.

1862 Following torrential rains, 75 die in Victoria's Great Avalanche.

1903 Seychelles separates from Mauritius.

1971 Airport opened by the Queen; tourism soars.

29 June 1976 Independence from Britain. James Mancham becomes President.

5 June 1977 Prime Minister Albert René's coup d'état.

1993 First multiparty elections.

2006 Opposition Leader Anglican priest Wavel Ramkalawan contests presidential election.

2005 onwards Arab Russian land/hotel investment.

the airport and later, in typically generous Seychelles fashion, pardoned. In a bid to end the paranoia about invasions and intrigue, René stepped up his rhetoric against the exiled 'Movement for the Resistance', which was dealt a mortal blow in 1985 when its talented young leader Gerard Hoarau fell to a mysterious assassin's bullet in a London street.

Political instability is never good for tourism. The economy started to sour, and some of René's lieutenants abandoned him. The influential Catholic Church intensified its criticism, and pressure mounted for a return to free elections. Wily as ever (touched, perhaps by De Quincy's spirit), René suddenly reversed direction and agreed to an election in 1993, only to knock the wind out of everyone's sails by winning 60% of the vote, and so retaining the Presidency.

Opposition was at least now legal, journalistic criticism allowed, and Mancham was back in Seychelles as leader of the opposition Democratic Party. René retired in 2004, albeit as a benevolent *eminence grise*, and was replaced by his former vice president James Michel. His new People's Party won 55% of the vote at the 2011 general election.

GOVERNMENT AND ECONOMY

Albert René's long if at times authoritarian rule as President (1977–2004) transformed Seychelles from an impoverished coconut colony a thousand miles from anywhere to an island country in which practically everyone has a job, a pension, access to free education, health facilities, and a government loan to build a home – benevolent and successful New Age socialism. But the old order changes, new wants emerge and René read the signs well. Free speech, press and elections have turned Seychelles into a flourishing democracy.

▼ *Below: Air Seychelles' inter-island Otter proudly displays its new colours.*

INTRODUCING SEYCHELLES

Economy

In pre-airport days of barefoot coconut collecting, colonial grants-in-aid, cinnamon, vanilla, and subsistence fishing, the average Seychellois was dirt poor. But tourism, tuna canning, construction and aggressive social planning have said goodbye to all that. 98% of the population is employed and the average GDP per capita is US$ 25,000. Everyone has a house, power, clean water, TV, landline, bank account, and many, a car. And a B&B. There are good tarred roads and a well-trained police force. Seychelles increasingly offers off-shore banking. 90% of the islands' requirements are imported and apart from tourism, there are very few industries (the brewery is the largest employer; 100 people) and not much in the way of exports other than canned tuna by the thousands of tonnes, coconut oil, sea cucumbers and a variety of spices. France, UK and Japan are the main export markets. There are no minerals although deep sea probes may one day produce oil and gas. Local wags will tell you that government inevitably boasts of possible Eureka finds at elections. Fuel and food-stuffs account for 50% of imports, including Parisian *patisserie* for gourmand visitors.

A Holiday Package

Once upon a time, the British India Steam Navigation liners would call monthly in Seychelles, and the occasional British warship would appear, show a film on Gordon Square (now Freedom Square) and play a football match against the local team. Until the airport was built in 1971 the Seychelles were the forgotten islands.

While the coming of tourism has exposed the Seychellois to prying cameras, consumer brand names, topless bathers and foreigners tramping through their Eden, the money is good and with few natural resources other than its beauty, its tuna canning and its people, it was always going to be one of the few industries Seychelles could exploit on any realistic economic scale. 70% of tourists come from Europe. The 2008 world

◄ *Left: Relaxing in front of the idyllic Indian Ocean Lodge, Praslin.*

economic fallout did not greatly impact, but Seychelles subsequently extended its marketing to the middle if not mass backpacker markets. However, high-end tourism sits squarely as the cornerstone of Seychelles' economy. In the need to attract investment and create employment, Seychelles is financially caught between reef and rough surf. It has managed to retain control of some 30% of its visitor accommodation and these are mainly small establishments. Of the large hotels (25 rooms or more) and coral island resorts, many are owned by foreign investors, mainly Maldivian, Malaysian, Mauritian, Arab, Russian and South African, resulting in high forex remittances. The coral island resorts, e.g. Denis Island and Bird, are by far the most appealing destinations. The large hotels, spas and resorts, a few with a density of over 200 rooms, are luxurious in a Brazilian telenova way but in spite of arrival champagne, wondrous foyers, and unbelievably stunning beaches they naturally lack the local charm and cuisine of the small hotels and family-run B&Bs that dot the islands. Some years there are over 190,000 tourists, the majority from European countries and now Russia and the Arab states.

INTRODUCING SEYCHELLES

Fishing

Surrounded by ocean and coral reef, fishing by handline, indigenous *kazye* trap and harpoon has always been Seychelles' primary harvest, diet and pastime. Some 4000 tonnes of fish are landed annually, while 400,000 tons of tuna caught by foreign vessels and trans-shipped in Mahé is, in an era of depleted tuna stocks, proving controversial. About 40,000 tonnes is canned locally, accounting for 90% of Seychelles exports. The factory is sited at the Fishing Port, Victoria, and when the wind blows southerly can be fishily smelt nearby. Giant clams – the blessing fonts you see as you enter the older churches – and very expensive black oyster pearls are also farmed for export.

Agriculture

To all those who dropped anchor in Seychelles' blue waters down the centuries, the islands were always regarded as a bountiful paradise. However, even Eden's natural resources suffered at the hands of those who came, as tortoises were curiosities, turtles a popular source of fresh meat and the tall trees highly valued as shipbuilding timber.

In general, the alkaline granite soil is not generous, and trying to grow anything on Seychelles for profit was at best a risky enterprise. Plantations of **copra, cinnamon, patchouli** and **vanilla** all enjoyed short-lived booms but the plantation owners or *grands blancs* seldom had the wherewithal to match their refined aspirations.

Seychellois are instinctive and innovative farmers. Everybody has a vegetable garden, fruit trees and where land is available, such as the carefully farmed Denis Island, there are homemade cheeses, bacon, duck eggs, even fresh milk, a luxury in Seychelles.

Tea from the slopes of Mahé's mountains supplies local requirements (try the *citronelle*). Seychelles is self-sufficient in chicken, beef, pigs and, for honeymooners' beds, wonderful flower arrangements. There are substantial vegetable farms on all the larger islands.

▼ *Below: These giant crayfish, in Kreol* omar *(lobster), can be blue or green.*

Brisk Business

Manufacturing and business in Seychelles have flourished albeit in a small way. Many businesses, such as restaurants and craft shops, benefit from the considerable spin-offs from tourism, but there are also architects, sculptors, artists, and gold jewellery-makers doing well. There are several daily full-colour tabloids in English, South African DSTV, and Seychelles Broadcasting Corporation (SBC). Being an island, shipping and tanker deliveries are prosperous concerns, while the presence of Cable and Wireless and their competitor, Airtel, has ensured an excellent and modern communication system. Seychelles appears in the *Guinness Book of Records* as being the smallest nation to run its own international airline.

▲ *Above: Everyone has a breadfruit in their back yard, some larger than others.*

Seychelles has offshore banking offering international trusts, mutual funds and ship registration. There are tax incentives for investors and a development bank for new projects. The conference centre in Victoria seats 600, a favourite with African states as Seychelles is considered safer.

Importing practically everything and being a touch casual about utilizing its own resources, Seychelles limits itself to producing beer, tea, tuna, black pearls and bottled spring water, while cigarettes, milk and fruit juices are reprocessed from imported stocks. Local plastic-packaged manioc and banana chips are marvellous. But other than oodles of palms, beaches and azure seas, there is nothing developing-world cheap about Seychelles. If you like bargaining, no harm in trying. The bank rate fluctuates around SR14/15 to US$ 1. Hotel rates can be different. There is no black market. For many years Seychelles quoted in Euros, but visitors no longer have to pay for services in forex. You won't find a McDonald's but a Seybrew costs US$5 in a hotel. The key remains whether tourism can be maintained to match the good life the Seychellois have come to accept as normal.

MARINE PARK ISLANDS

There are six islands in the Ste Anne Marine Park off Victoria: the pyramid-shaped **Ste Anne** (the largest), **Cerf** (everyone's favourite Sunday picnic island), **Round, Long, Moyenne** and **Caché** (Hidden). There are six inner island resorts, a short boat ride away, several very posh. Among the non-hotel restaurants, a special one is the quixotic Jolly Roger's on the Robinson Crusoe, Moyenne island. You can walk round Round Island in 15 minutes. Each island has its own distinctive flavour and exquisite off-shore corals.

INTRODUCING SEYCHELLES

THE PEOPLE

Western writers have always described the Seychellois as smiling, happy-go-lucky folk straight out of a Gauguin painting. Nonsense. The Seychellois certainly know and take advantage of the paradise in which they live, and the climate and beauty make them fairly laid-back, but they are not beaming, brown-skinned natives in sarongs singing love songs as the long boats ride in on the surf. They are canny, wily, island folk 'with one thousand virtues and a few hundred vices' as former President Mancham wrote in his poem. Drawn from African, Malagasy, Indian, Chinese, and European roots, they have developed a unique and adaptable culture with a great sense of fun and an irrepressible knack for gossiping – at every bus stop, street corner and shop.

The Seychellois can be welcoming, quick to offer help or to invite you home for a meal, and happy to share their knowledge of the islands. Tourism has changed their lives, but it has not trampled their spirit. At the least hint of arrogance or condescension they will freeze you out, but the welcome in hotels, initially a touch hesitant, is soon exuberant and tinged with humour.

▼ *Below: Tin shops perch precariously on the roadside at Quatre Bornes.*

Family Life

Coming out of the times when there were no priests, slaves were not allowed to marry (their children automatically belonged to the master) and in any event a wedding feast was prohibitive, a tradition of living *en ménage* (together) without marrying took root. Families tend to be rather loose arrangements. The many children 'born on the outside' are commonly looked after by their mother alone. **Seychellois women** are confident, shrewd, and often the fulcrum of society. There are proportionately more women in the Seychelles parliament than in any other country, and they are often the power behind many businesses.

▲ *Above: Colourful gear,* de rigueur *for basketball guys.*

Language

There is really no such thing as a Kreol person in Seychelles. 'Creoles' live in Louisiana. Everyone is Seychellois, and their language is **Kreol**, sometimes written 'Creole', based on the French of plantation days, but it has strong African intonations and has, over the years, incorporated a good many English words, Malagasy, Indian, Arabic, and more recently, truncated hip-hop speak. A French speaker will understand it, although to read it in its written form is mind-boggling.

USEFUL KREOL EXPRESSIONS

Knowing a few words of Kreol will always win you friends:
Good morning, sir • *bonzour msye* (pronounce it phonetically)
Where's the road, brother? • *Oli semen, mon frer?* (From old French: *Où est le chemin, mon frère?*)
Please, madam, what time does the bus get here? • *Pardon, madam, ou capab di mwa, keler bis yarive?* (Roughly from old French: *Pardon, madame, quand est-ce que arrive le bus ici?*)
May I use your toilet, please? • *Mwan kapab servi ou kabinen silvouple?*
Is there a shop over there? • *I annan en laboutik laba?*
I am going to ... • *Mon pe al kot ...*
Excuse me • *Eskiz mwan*
Yes, no • *wi, non*
Do you speak English, madam? • *Ou koz Angle, madam?*
Hotel • *lotel*
I don't know • *mon pa konnen*
How much? • *konbyen sa?*
One, two, three • *enn, de, twa*
And, everyone's favourite words in Kreol:
kouyon • expletive – used liberally to cover every volatile situation, self-recrimination and motoring confrontation.
Bouldou or *kwaver* • sweetheart or knee-trembler.

INTRODUCING SEYCHELLES

Kreol is also spoken in Mauritius and in parts of the Caribbean, but Seychelles was the first country to develop it as a written medium and give it equal status as an official language. It is a living, changing language, and a Kreol Institute has been set up in Mahé to promote it. Primary school children used to be taught in Kreol although this has changed to English. Business and law use English, those of French descent speak that language at home, and the news is read on television in all three.

Religion

The **Catholic** faith, to which 89% of the population are adherents, remains at the core of Seychellois culture. The menfolk, except at funerals, affect to treat that bond lightly, but there is no doubting the strength of it, and one of the images of the islands is the colourfully dressed worshippers on their way to Sunday Mass – men in starched white shirts, the older ladies with hats, and the young girls in their lovingly sewn first communion dresses.

Inside church, with the scent of eau de cologne and coconut oil wafting under the fans, the atmosphere is heady. The singing is excellent, especially at churches served by the increasing number of young Seychellois priests, while features such as the marquetry interior of Our Lady of Seven Sorrows at Anse Boileau and the impressive altar windows of the rebuilt Anglican cathedral in Victoria lift the spirit.

There are beautiful grottoes along every remote road in Seychelles, and the church bell tower is the focal point of each tiny village. Many islanders still cross themselves passing a church if they're in a bus. Saints' feast days are grand events, especially La Digue's *fête Assomption* on 15 August, with bunting, sports competitions, feasting, music and processions.

Other religions and denominations do have a presence. There are four Anglican churches in Seychelles; in Victoria there is a new Hindu temple and a mosque; and there are also smart Jehovah's Witness, Seventh Day Adventist and a 700-seater Pentecostal Assembly Church. In the days before electricity there was substantial belief in *bonnonm dibwa's grigri* (black magic), but with a young modern population it mainly exists today as effective herbalism, folk memory and party banter.

◄ *Opposite: Every faith flourishes in Seychelles, such as Baha'í near the schooner quay in Praslin.*
▼ *Below: A wayside shrine on a country road bears witness to the islands' Roman Catholic heritage.*

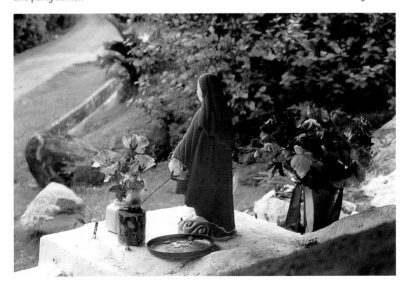

INTRODUCING SEYCHELLES

▼ *Below: Sega dancing – sensual, striking, and straight from the deeply rooted Kreol tradition.*

Music and Dance

There are photographic, political biograhy, historical, and advertisement-rich guidebooks on Seychelles. But apart from the mischievous Soungoula stories, Glynn Burridge's *Kolony* and Paul Tingay's novels, there is very little literature. The lush tropical atmosphere of Seychelles has always been an inspiration for artists, but it is music that truly captures the spirit of the islands, and no more so than the defiant, evocative *moutya*. High in the mountains or on a remote beach a slow chanting and sensuous shuffle dance would begin around a fire made from dry coconut fronds, a line of men facing another of women, everyone else watching. Born in slave days, the *moutya* is pure Africa, the rumbling drum evoking anguished memories of another time. It was frowned upon by the establishment, who were seldom invited to the all-night rave-ups, and naughty children would get a hiding from parents for sneaking a peak. These days, to save milady's blushes, visitors are treated to a considerably refined version at hotel dinners and folk festivals.

The sega comes from the Sri Lankan *Baila*, the playing of which is no longer allowed in buses (together with loud talking, the notice reads). It is danced in colourful Mauritian costumes. The islanders' (and some would say more wicked) version is danced with small, rhythmic steps and a much subtler sway to the hips, neither partner ever touching.

Family dances and weddings are jolly affairs, with violins, banjo, accordion, triangle and drums providing the music for *kamtole* – Seychelles waltzes, polkas, masok and contredanse, performed with shouted instructions from a *komander*, rather like country and western.

Leading musicians in Seychelles include Patrick Victor, a *moutya* poet and folk singer, classically trained David André (his *nostalgie* music with Xu Lu's violin is exquisite), Jenny Letourdi, Antoinette Dodin (*Perdi maman, perdi tou*) and you must not leave Seychelles without seeing the dancing and music of Kevin Valentin Sokwe's *moutya* and sega group. Sophisticated, sensual, superb.

No-one, however, has reached the standing of old folk hero Tonpa, legendary master of the Seychelles *bonm* (bow and gourd). Above the fountain at La Bastille Archives in Victoria there is a bust of Tonpa and two friends on the *zez, bonm* and *tambour* (drum), playing, as Victor's *moutya* song goes, '...until dawn breaks, and it's time to milk the goats'.

Island Cuisine

With a heritage drawing from French, Indian, Chinese and Kreol roots, the quality of the cuisine in Seychelles could only be wonderful. Few menus fail to be mouth-watering. The staples of the Seychellois diet are *kordonnyen* fish, rice, coconut, breadfruit, chillies, spices and mangoes, each of them cooked in a hundred different and delicious ways. Indian dal or yellow lentils are commonly made into a thick soup, while saffron rice is served with an onion, orange and spices salad as a picnic pilau with grilled suckling pig. Various types of seafood are always popular, among them grilled *bourzwa* snapper fish, cold *zob* fish, and fresh *tectec* clams – dug up from the beach, and then made into a soup. Other delicacies of the islands are *satini rekin* (dried shark chutney), smoked sailfish and fruit bat, but perhaps nothing beats the simplest rice and salted fish in a banana frond pouch, fisherman style.

▼ Below: Karang is a good catch and delicious.

INTRODUCING SEYCHELLES

▶ *Right: Island cuisine is often decorated with exquisite flowers.*
▶▶ *Opposite: Thrills and paragliding spills at Beau Vallon beach.*

For dessert, go for bananas fried in brown sugar or pineapple in red wine. A few of the other delights are manioc (cassava) as a pudding cooked in freshly grated coconut, sweet potatoes in honey, or wild *framboises* from the mountains of La Misère. Sweets are made of *pamplemousse* peel, jams from *zamalak* fruit, and popular snacks are *gato pimen* chillibites and nougat coco. The local beers are pretty ordinary. Wines are super expensive. Try *kalou* (coconut tree toddy), or, for a real blast, *baka kann* rum. Lemon grass or *citronelle* tea helps the digestion. Check your coffee; avoid the imported instant sachet stuff. If the opportunity arises, never turn up the chance of home cooking.

Sport and Recreation

People tend to wake up with the six o'clock sun, so wild all-hours revelling is not common, though hotels with their discos, casinos, coffee shops and barbecues have replaced much of the home entertainment, which is usually folksy accordion singsongs and dancing. After church on Sunday, the done thing is a crate of Seybrew, ghetto blaster and giggle with the gals picnic to Port Launay or Anse La Mouche beaches.

Sitting on an upturned bucket in a village back yard to the ferocious slapping of dominoes is a regular rite all through the islands. It is universally addictive among men-folk, along with football (35 teams) and athletics. There is an annual week-long Kreol Festival at the end of October, an underwater Festival of the Sea (SUBIOS), regular *bazars* in every village and the 40km (25-mile) windsurfing race to Praslin. *Mind the barracudas, dear.*

In Seychelles everyone is a fisherman, and making friends with the *pêcheur* nearest to your particular beach could avoid the cost of big sea charters. Golf is played at the Reef golf course – where the hazards include falling coconuts and crabs with a reputation for stealing balls – and at Lémuria resort on Praslin. You can also ride horses at Barbarons and La Digue, paraglide or jetski noisily at Beau Vallon, and find all the regular water sports at most big hotels.

OCTOPUS CURRY

Octupus curry is the national dish of Seychelles. Wash the octopus and beat the poor old fellow with a rolling pin for 15 minutes, then boil (flesh must remain soft). Slice the flesh very finely. Season with two teaspoons of curry powder, pepper, salt, two onions, a touch of chilli and two cinnamon leaves. Add three cups of coconut cream and cook for 30 minutes. Serve with rice and heart of palm salad (also called 'millionaire's salad', as it takes the centre of one palmiste palm to make each salad).

2
North Mahé

Mahé is the largest of the widely spread islands of Seychelles, only 27km (17 miles) long but given an impressive presence by a backbone of high forested mountains. These granitic peaks are the highest in the archipelago, and a distinguishing feature since they were first sighted by Arab seamen. Mahé was the site of the first French landings in 1742, and the first settlement in 1770. Today 87% of the population of Seychelles lives on the island, with a large proportion of that figure in the nation's capital, **Victoria** (population 27,000).

Around Mahé's coastline there are 75 beaches and coves (known as 'anse' in Seychelles), ranging from long, sweeping stretches of sand to isolated little bays tucked among granite cliffs and thick green forest. Except for the western corner, a narrow and twisting tarred road rings the island; it fringes sea, reef and an overgrown coconut jungle dotted with green- and red-tiled homes and precariously perched general stores.

The side of Mahé to the northeast of the central range of mountains encompasses the three most important single locations on the island: the **airport** at Point La Rue, the capital, Victoria, and **Beau Vallon Bay**, the principal tourist area. Victoria is the main harbour in Seychelles, and the heart of business and commerce. It rises quickly into the mountains, through leafy suburbs such as Bel Air and Bel Eau. Driving north, the land soon becomes more rural, albeit fringed by land reclamation islands and their now lush

CLIMATE

The sea and winds keep Mahé refreshed. **Humidity** is around 80% all year. To some extent, the buildings and paved roads of Victoria hold in the heat and make it hotter than the rural and mountain areas. **Temperature** is 29°C (84°F) year-round, with only a slight drop at night. **Rain** falls heavily from November through January but drops to as low as 50mm (2in) in July.

◄ *Opposite: A stormy rainbow on Le Niol heights overlooking Beau Vallon.*

NORTH MAHÉ

Don't Miss

★★★ Beau Vallon Beach: the definitive Seychelles beach, 15 minutes from Victoria.

★★★ Victoria Walkabout: start at the Clock Tower, and take in all the sights, sounds and smells of the capital.

★★★ Ste Anne Marine National Park: just off Victoria, a feast of coral and fish. See it from the comfort of a glass semi-submersible.

★★ Botanical Gardens: a downtown taste of the spectacular Seychelles flora, coco de mer, tortoises and lunch.

★★ The Market: everything exotic for sale and some great personalities.

★★ Game Fishing: boats from Marine Charter next to the yacht club.

★ Natural History Museum: near Clock Tower; 43 original Marianne North paintings. 1m wide clam shell.

★ National Cultural Centre, Historical Museum and Art Gallery: near Le Chantier fountain roundabout.

casuarinas. The first 'whispering palms' and rumbling reef are at North East Point. Mahé's top beach, Beau Vallon, is only a 15-minute drive over the mountain saddle from Victoria, while huddled in the wide bay of the eastern coastline are a group of small islands that are incorporated in **Ste Anne Marine National Park**, a kaleidoscopic if threatened garden of underwater life.

VICTORIA

From the air or the sea Victoria seems to be lost in a green jungle beneath the towering black cliffs of Trois Frères. The first French inhabitants were attracted to the sheltered anchorage, but the land must have seemed an impenetrable swathe of mangrove swamp. The settlement was initially called L'Etablissement, before becoming Victoria in 1841 in honour of the Queen. It is the seat of government, the location of most of the main institutions and businesses, and the only centre in the 115 islands that can really be described as a town.

Victoria's size has been substantially increased in recent years by land reclamation, which has allowed the development of the New Port, the airport, a large tuna cannery, a sports complex, new factories, and clusters of high-density flats. The new double highway to the airport enables cars to reach 80kph (50mph). Still, it is one of the smallest capitals in the world – you can stroll from one end of town to the other in 20 minutes. Buses and pedestrians dodge and weave through the town's narrow streets. Colourful, corrugated iron chateaux with drooping balconies stand defiantly beside chunky modern buildings, while along the tree-lined pavements life bustles with street stalls, music and closely packed general stores.

A Walk around the Clock ★★★

Victoria is small enough that it doesn't take long to see everything on foot. You quickly pick up the chirpiness of the Seychellois and the relaxed tropical feel of the place. The focal point of town is the **Clock Tower**, erected in 1903 to mark Seychelles' coming of age as a separate colony. Before land reclamation it marked the old harbour shore. During the 2004 tsunami, waters swept up to the base of the clock. One wag reckoned he even saw a shark.

Starting at the Clock Tower, set off along Francis Rachel – it was named after one of the insurgents killed during the coup d'état of 1977. An avenue of shady trees and flowers runs past the gracious 1887 courthouse opposite Temooljies with its bust of Pierre Poivre (Peter Pepper) who in 1772 introduced his namesake, pepper, and all spices nice to Seychelles. The timber and tin-roofed shops such as Adam Moosa and Chaka Brothers have, fortunately, been preserved. These are general stores date back 100 years when they were the islands' bankers, offering 'indefinite credit and unfailing courtesy'. Their sons and grandsons still greet you with old-world politesse as you enter, even if you can no longer buy a bottle of home-made lemonade with a marble stopper. The local crafts kiosks, formerly enlivening the clock tower, are now beneath the trees of Fiennes Esplanade.

The ultramodern facilities of Cable and Wireless are alongside the old grey and white colonial façade of **Kenwyn House**, a national monument. Nearby is the **Mosque** of Sheik Mohamed bin Khalifa. Carry on past the **National Library, Historical Museum, Archives** and **Art Gallery** with its Grecian columns and you come to the huge dark trees marking **Le Chantier** fountain and roundabout, site of the old boat-building yard and today gateway to **New Port** and the airport road.

▲ *Above: The Victorian Clock Tower, in memory of Her Majesty, 'Empress of India'.*
◄ *Opposite: Facing Victoria harbour, reclaimed stretches hope one day to compete with the lovely islands beyond.*

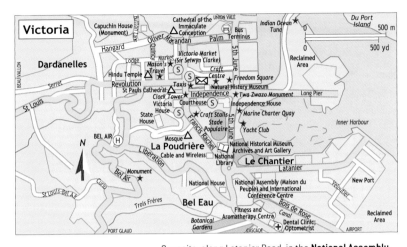

Opposite, along Latanier Road, is the **National Assembly**, or *Maison du Peuple*, and **International Conference Centre**, partly hidden by trees, and beyond it the power station and port office. Continue the walk by doubling back along 5th June Avenue (the day of the coup in 1977, Liberation Day) towards the town centre, passing a children's playground, then the **yacht club**, with halyards clattering in the breeze. Here the Rousseau-chained " Zom Libre " has been liberated and replaced by a Delacroix "Liberty" fountain. The Twa Zwazo roundabout nearby, a sculpture of soaring fairy terns, defines the start of tree-lined Independence Avenue running past Pirates Arms. The hard-drinking '*grand blancs*' plantocracy used to tipple here or at the long gone colonial Seychelles Club opposite; *Le Peuple* at the Baka Club across the football ground. The Silvery Clock Tower is the town centre, post office on the corner, State House towards the mountain.The narrow shop-lined street leading past the taxi rank to the market on the left and Catholic Cathedral dead ahead may soon be a pedestrian mall with its 100 year old tin houses carefully preserved. Behind you Independence Avenue leads to the fishing port and tuna factory. Veer left for the inter-island ferry terminal, looking out on Cerf Passage, wind generators and the islands in Ste Anne's Marine Park.

WHERE THE CLOCK CHIMES TWICE

There is a clock that chimes in Victoria, but it isn't the Clock Tower in the middle of town. A crucial part was lost over the side of the ship as the commemorative clock was unloaded in 1903, and no-one could make the bell work after that. What you will hear chiming is the clock in the Roman Catholic Cathedral, beyond the market. When the travel writer Alec Waugh (brother of the novelist Evelyn) came to Seychelles, he wrote a book called *Where the Clock Chimes Twice*. And why does it chime twice? One version is that the first is to wake everyone up, and the second to tell them the time.

The old B.I. ships of yesteryear used to anchor out in the roads, where in earlier days young men would dive 18m (60ft) to the sea bed to retrieve thrown coins.

Natural History Museum *

The tiny Natural History Museum next door to the post office, and once the venerable Carnegie Library, is one of the few old wide-staircase buildings that has survived. Seychelles has 1000 marine fish species, 450 species of molluscs, 100 different types of hard corals, nine different types of breeding terns, giant tortoises, freshwater terrapins and turtles. The wolf snake is the most distinctive of Seychelles' three non-poisonous types. Tiny sooglossid frogs hide up the mountains, lizards clamp on ceilings and bright green geckos on trees. The 700 beetle types include the endemic giant tenebrionid beetle. There are 766 species of flowering plants and 85 ferns on the granitic islands, and 350 types of seaweed. The pride of Seychelles is the coco de mer. You can learn about all this biodiversity by strolling around the museum's cabinets and displays. Upstairs are Marianne North's 43 magnificent flower and plant paintings of Seychelles 130 years ago. The rest are in Kew Gardens, London. (Open Monday–Friday and Saturday mornings.)

National Cultural Centre *

Built by public subscription, it combines the National Library, recently renovated National Museum, Art Gallery and National Archives. The building itself belongs to a school of architecture which can only be described as tropic gothic – Grecian columns and soaring space. There are permanent exhibitions on slavery and the British colonial rule that ended it. Look out for pirates' pistols, old Seychellois musical

▼ Below: The elegant National Cultural Centre.

NORTH MAHÉ

SEYCHELLES ARTISTS

The islands can boast a garland of excellent artists.
- **Michael Adams.** Colour, people and activity. Much imitated.
- **Jeanne D'Offay.** Oils. Island scenes.
- **Tom Bowers.** Bronze sensual figures.
- **Christine Harter.** Watercolours of rural Seychelles.
- **Serge Rouillon.** Little houses tucked in greenery.
- **Verney Cresswell.** Beach scenes.
- **Leon Bacco.** Woodcarvings.
- **Gerard Devoud.** Local life paintings. Prints exhibited world wide.
- **Daniel Monthy.** Works with bamboo and indigenous fibres. There are art studios around every corner in Seychelles.

instruments, Mahé in Victorian days, shipwrecks, portraits of historical Seychelles stalwarts and the 1841 bust of Queen Victoria (supposedly the world's smallest) which used to grace the drinking fountain outside the Courthouse. Even more fascinating is the 1756 Possession Stone, the symbol of French claim to the islands, and another, an old pirate's tombstone inscribed, with skull and crossbones, which reads: 'Jean-Pierre Le Chartier, killed on March 4, 1805 by his friend Evellon. Passers-by pray for me'. Whether for pirate or his murderer is left unsaid.

Inside, it is lovely. There are not a great many books, but it has an unhurried reference department, and it is a wonderful home for Seychelles art. The building is also home to the Legislative Assembly.

Shopping

The craft kiosks along Fiennes Esplanade sell local shopping bags, beach wraps, hats of coconut fibre, postcards and souvenirs. Try to avoid the pretty seashells. They look better untouched, underwater. 'Tortoiseshell' items made from the shell of hawksbill turtles was a fine art in Seychelles years ago. Now it is forbidden. Near the Clock Tower is Lakaz Cooperative selling local crafts and in the

Pirates Arms arcade, Antik Colony. The Post Office has a philatelic bureau.

There is a good bookshop, Antigone, maps at the Survey Office and, still in Independence Avenue, airline offices and photo shops. Past the new Anglican Cathedral you come to Camion Hall (after the camions or trucks, Seychelles' first buses that parked here as did long gone rickshas). The arcade shops include a

Duty Free, Kreolor's gold and local black oyster pearl jewellery, and opticians *Ou Linet* (your specs). There are at least five Internet cafés, 13 estate agents, flower shops, and seven banks (ATMs). Also in Albert Street is the Sooty Tern, selling works of three local artists. The STC Supermarket is not Waitrose. In pre-revolutionary days it belonged to Founding President Mancham's family. Seychellois Presidents, ex and extant are literary souls with biographies galore.

In Revolution Avenue, where the terrible avalanche of 1862 swept down, is the police station opposite Mason's Travel, the first tour operator in Seychelles.

Market Street, a pedestrian mall, is the shopping hub for Seychelles housewives. The little shops sell everything from local music to iPhones. On the corner you will find Kanti's rickety multi-storey tin-roofed shop. Now gone to higher debates, Kanti was a much-loved Seychelles conversationalist; man for all seasons.

Victoria Market ★★

The action-packed market is hard to miss under its elegant new roof and courtyard mango trees in Market Street. Started in 1839, it is still called the Sir Selwyn-Clarke Market after the medical doctor and post-World War II Governor. It is open every day except Sunday, with Saturday being particularly hectic. The best time to be there is when the fish are heaved in.

The market is a hive of all things strange and exotic. You can buy *bourzwa* red snapper heads for soup, pale green chilli-like *sousout*, or *patole* (a sort of hollow cucumber), *zamalak* fruits, mangoes (ripe or unripe), *fatak* reed brooms,

▲ *Above: Sunshine or rain, there is always something interesting to buy at Victoria's market.*
◀ *Opposite: The Clock Tower (rare 1939 painting by Émile Hugon).*

BEST BUYS

- **Baskets, bags and hats.** Palm weave.
- **Black oyster pearls.** From Praslin.
- **Gold jewellery** weaved into local cowries, coconut shell and mother-of-pearl.
- ***Moutya* music.** Patrick Victor, Jany Letourdie, David André, Jean Marc Volcy.
- **Island paintings.** A dozen artists. Superb.
- **Spices.** Cinnamon sticks, nutmeg, *Karambol* jam, wild honey in the market.
- **Takamaka Bay rum.** *Grandpère* D'Offay's secret recipe.
- **Perfumes.** Kreolfleurage (now rare) from exotic spices and flowers.

NORTH MAHÉ

coconut graters, and chillies, the smaller the hotter.

The best part of the market, however, is near the back where some wonderful characters keep their stalls. See if you can track down Lolo Adrienne's bottled jams and chutneys. He will explain with all the tricks and treats of a medicine man how to cook with his special curry powders and hellfire sauces. Or try speaking a few words of Kreol to Yvonne Sidoney at her fruit, vegetable and *gallette mayok* (a crusty biscuit made of manioc) stall, and you'll make a lifelong friend. Shoo away the white egrets, which are called *Madam Paton* by the locals (after a white-haired lady who bore a resemblance), as you taste some of the wonderful delicacies.

The Botanical Gardens ★★

Industrial wealth, a far-flung empire and botanist Charles Darwin's studies on evolution caused an explosion of interest in birds and bees in Victorian Britain. One outcome was Kew Gardens in London; another – if not quite so grand – was the Botanical Gardens in Seychelles.

The entrance to the Botanical Gardens is less than a mile south of town parallel with the road leading up to the hospital. Coco de mer palms dominate the path up into the Gardens. Others of the islands' six endemic palms to be found there include *latanier*, which is used for thatching, and *palmiste*, the favourite ingredient for millionaire's salad.

The Gardens lie in a granite-humped, grassy strip between two small streams trickling down from the massif that soars above the trees. Water lilies, papyrus, and even some tiny fish and transparent shrimps can be spotted here. The 6ha (15-acre) Gardens were established over 100 years ago and owe a lot to their original Director, Paul Rivaltz Dupont, who travelled the world gathering exotic trees and plants. Many of the unusual trees are labelled. There is a nursery for young plants, an orchid garden with samples of these exotic blooms from all over the world, a Seychelles giant tortoise pen formed by natural black boulders, and

VICTORIA'S VICTORIANA

• Kenwyn House on Francis Rachel Street. Beside Cable and Wireless.
• Queen Victoria's Diamond Jubilee fountain. The porcelain original is in the museum.
• Clock Tower, 1903. Originally painted black.
• Old tin-roofed buildings of the Promenade opposite Fiennes Esplanade (after the 1918 Governor) along Francis Rachel Street.
• St Paul's Anglican Cathedral, 1857. The old bell tower was incorporated into the new 2004 church.
• Roman Catholic Cathedral where the clock chimes twice, 1862.
• Marie Antoinette Restaurant at the top of Revolution Avenue.
• State House, 1913. Classical Raj colonial grandeur.
• Court House. Until 1923, it was Seychelles' hospital.
• Hospital, 1924. Double-storey iron filigree and airy verandahs.

a thatched café, *Le Sapin*, set like its namesake beneath Norfolk pines. Up the hill you might find fruit bats hanging upside down from the trees. There are over 30 palm types in the Gardens, and some 70 tree species including jackfruit, pink-flowered cannonball, teak and nutmeg, the seeds of which schoolboys heat by rubbing them against granite and then apply to unsuspecting chums' legs. The Gardens (entrance fee, open daily) are the Headquarters of Seychelles' National Botanical Gardens Foundation.

Cemetery

Three kilometres (2 miles) from town along the road to the south is Seychelles' main cemetery. Cemeteries may not be a common choice for a stroll, but this one has such an attractive swathe of bumpy grass, black granite and open mountain scenery that it deserves being the exception. Turn uphill in Mont Fleuri just before the old white coral wall and park. If it is near All Saints' (public holiday) and All Souls' Day (November 1 and 2), you'll see brightly coloured flowers on the black granite tombstones, time-worn mausoleums and newly whitewashed crosses that drift up the hill to the mountains above.

The inscriptions on the tombstones are often in French

STATE HOUSE

Completed in 1913, this gracious residence of colonial governors and presidents is sited on a small rise just above town. The house and manicured lawns were designed by Lady William Davidson, the wife of one of the governors. She neglected to include in her design a staircase for the two-storeyed house, a fact that was only discovered mid-construction. It has lofty white columns, two-storey high ceilings, polished floors, discreet staff and split cane roll-down blinds on the verandah where in colonial days *punkah-wallah* wafted luncheons would be held for those who signed the Visitors' Book. Access is by permission only. Queau de Quincy's tomb is in the grounds.

NORTH MAHÉ

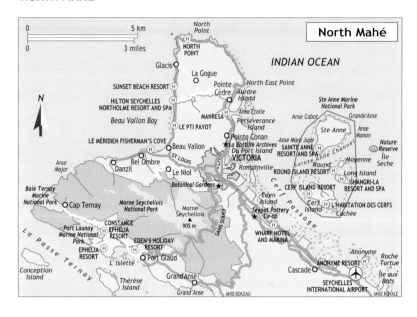

North Mahé

GriGri Ghosts

In the 19th century (and perhaps a touch today) there was *Ti-Albert* voodoo herbalism, *dandosya* zombies (who will call if you sweep your yard after sunset), spells, chicken bones under pillows and tarot cards cast by the *bonnonm dibwa*, the old fellow of the woods. *Grigri* magic (if a *katiti*, or kestrel, roosts in your roof someone is going to die) adds that spicy touch for visitors and Seychelles is only too happy to exploit this attraction. They'll even produce a *nam* (ghost) for you in the old settlers' graveyard above Victoria where a 2.7m (9ft) 'giant' walks around his tomb. It was last seen by a tourist. Naturally.

– the language always reserved for formal occasions – but Kreol is found too on the little white home-made crosses.

From the road at the top of the cemetery there is a scenic walk back to town. It runs past Rochon, where women used to wash clothes in the river, slapping them against boulders and holding raucous conversations across from one level to the next. Under a tangled spaghetti of electricity and telephone wires, festooned with the webs of giant black and brown golden orb spiders, mynah birds yabber away as noisily as Paradise FM. A narrow footbridge beneath a dark canopy of trees crosses into the aptly named Forêt Noire (Black Forest). Not far beyond the forest there are views of the emerald waters of the harbour, with large boats anchored around the docks, and Ste Anne's Island beyond.

To complete the walk, cut left up Liberation Road just before National House to Bel Eau which seems steep until you come to another grand vista of the town. From here it is no more than a 15-minute walk back into town.

AROUND VICTORIA
Coastal Road South

A double highway damaged in the 2004 tsunami is the quickest route south from Victoria. But the old main road still twists past greenery, houses, tuck shops, brewery, reclaimed islands and lagoons. Tata buses thunder past, but a pleasant option is to walk it.

After the cemetery at **Mont Fleuri** you'll come to the **La Misère** mountain pass roundabout. Staying on the coast road you pass the church of **St Thérèse, Gerard Devoud's art gallery,** the **Seypot Pottery co-op,** the derelict schooner (and former restaurant) *Isle of Farquhar,* and then the bridge across the small **Mamelles River.** This used to mark the beginning of town, the start of dim streetlights and tarred road where you put on your shoes for the big city. It is also the site of the oldest plantation house in the islands, the elegant **Chateau des Mamelles.** Built in 1804, and formerly the residence of 'Le Corsair' Jean François Hodoul, it is now a national monument.

Past the busy Seychelles **brewery** is **Souverains des Mers,** where there is an exhibition of 40 model ships.

AVALANCHE

On the night of 12 October 1862 a terrifying tropical cyclone-driven avalanche descended on Victoria, with 100-tonne granite blocks rolling down the mountains, followed by a sea of mud which killed 80 people. For many years after, Seychelles measured time 'before or after the *Grande l'Avalasse*'. It destroyed Port Victoria, creating a flat area of ground which became the town's football field, Gordon Square (after General 'Chinese' Gordon), now Freedom Square.

▼ *Below:* Twa Zwazo, or *Three Birds Monument, symbolizes the fusion of Africa, Europe and Asia in the Seychelles people.*

NORTH MAHÉ

▼ *Below: The area around Cascade's old church was badly damaged in the 2004 Indian Ocean tsunami.*

Cascade

The alternative route from Victoria is along the new **Bois de Rose Avenue**, past the Roche Caiman housing estate which is not exactly blessed with architectural eloquence, but has a lovely little Nature Seychelles bird sanctuary nearby. The Wharf Marina's penthouse and moored cruisers give solace to gilded yachties. The afternoon wind whips the waves while across the road, small *katyolos* lie at anchor in the serpentine lagoon that borders the garden walls. Hardwoods are being planted along this road — which rapidly becomes Seychelles' only double highway — to supercede the forest of casuarinas that bond the coral rubble landfill.

Find a spot to get off the road and there are lovely views of mountain and mangrove shore. Watch for fiddler crabs at low tide. Red-steepled Cascade Church with its crumbling water mill, waterfall and pool is clearly visible not far from the double highway bridge swept away by the 2004 tsunami. In the old days Cascade was the choice mackerel fishing venue. Today you can almost touch Air Seychelles' new Airbus A320 as it roars in to touch down at the airport on reclaimed land just ahead.

The elegant 1882 church (built originally as a wooden chapel) dominates Cascade water village and its precipitous lagoon-flanking causeway, the old road.

Northern Peninsula

The road north from Victoria winds past **Radio Seychelles, La Bastille's ramparts**, and the now closed **Christian Broadcasting Station** (FEBA) with its red and white aerials marching out to sea. At **Anse Etoile**, during World War II, British troops were quartered and although a bunker still juts defiantly out to sea, the Nazi sub-

◀ *Left: Great granite boulders provide an artist's frame to many a cove in the islands.*

marines never came. Part of the bay was nicknamed 'smelly corner' after a U-shaped cove was filled in with refuse; it is now fully reclaimed.

Look back from the road approaching this northern peninsula of Mahé and the whole central massif is visible, with palm-framed views of Victoria town, the brooding **Trois Frères** mountain range, the busy port, and across the bay to the coral reefs around Ste Anne's Island.

The reef at **North East Point** is closer to the shore than at any other beach in Seychelles. If you want to take a closer look, wear a pair of shoes and explore it at low tide. Otherwise take a stroll along the shell-strewn beach with its fringe of palms and casuarinas. The bay is not particularly good for swimming, but there is a lovely wildness about the area, exposed as it is to the ocean and both seasons' monsoon winds.

There is an alternate narrow metal drive, up through forest and breadfruits then down past the cemetery to link up with the main circular road at the 1882 Church of St John the Baptist at Glacis on the western side of the island. The road begins opposite Pointe Cedre in Anse Etoile near the school and St Antoine church. The route is named after Seychelles' main reservoir, La Gogue, unfortunately not accessible to the public. There are two little villages in the hills, **Maldive** and **La Gogue**, each with a cluster of bread-fruit, mango and palm trees. Glacis is named after the giant

BEAUTY AND THE BEACH

- Best swimming beach on Mahé: Beau Vallon Bay.
- Best surfing beach: Grand'Anse, Mahé.
- Best snorkelling beach: Port Launay (Marine Park).
- Best fly-fishing (saltwater bonefish): the lagoon, Alphonse atoll.
- Most photographed: Anse Source d'Argent, La Digue.
- Voted World's Best Beach: ten times. Anse Lazio, Praslin.
- Best hideaway beaches: Petite Boileau Mahé and Anse La Blague, Praslin.
- Dangerous beaches May–October on Mahé: Grand'Anse, Anse Takamaka and Anse Intendance.
And on La Digue: Grand and Petite Anse.

▲ *Above: The exquisite azure, turquoise and emerald green hues of Ste Anne Marine National Park.*

▶ *Opposite: Beau Vallon Bay, as pure as it gets.*

SILENT WORLD

Ghostly rays, angelfish, tiger cowries and a treasure trove of corals await the snorkeler merely by swimming offshore around the many islands of Seychelles. Go in two's, and the first tip is to spit in your mask to prevent misting. But you can also learn to dive with aqualungs at 22 dive centres, many rated PADI 5★. You'll start in a swimming pool before progressing to one of the 40 excellent sites around Mahé or even the gorgeous 'Desroches Drop' plateau in the Amirantes. The professional may play at depth with a spotted 15m (49ft) whale shark but the amateur could easily swim with a turtle off Bird Island.

weathered granite boulders that fall steeply to the sea along this stretch of coast. You can park at Manresa if you want to walk.

STE ANNE MARINE NATIONAL PARK ★★★

The largest of Mahé's offshore islands are the group facing Victoria within the boundary of Ste Anne Marine National Park. **Ste Anne's**, a mountain pyramid of an island right in front of Victoria harbour, was the site of the first French settlement in 1770. In those days the island was surrounded by mangroves, crocodiles roamed its forests, and dugongs swam off its quiet shores. It has been declared a private island to protect the marine park and, no doubt, to encourage exclusivity for the new 87-villa resort. Contact the Marine Parks Authority for landing permission and fees. A whaling station was set up there in 1832, and during World War II, a giant petroleum storage tank to service seaplanes. Visitors coming in to land at the airport have one of the best views of the park. The water is a kaleidoscope of blue, turquoise, opal and aquamarine amongst the coral reefs, submarine islands of seaweed and the open flats of white sand which fringe these pretty islands.

The waters of the park are shallow, safe, and rich in coral and sea life. The best underwater areas for fish and coral are off Anse Cimitière and Cabot on Ste Anne, and in a stretch running between **Moyenne** and **Round Island**. The park and its islands are popular for day trips, with up to 35,000 people visiting it annually. One of the most interesting ways to see the spectacular underwater scenery is to sail the *Anahita* Reef Safari, which includes a semi-submersible, enabling you to see 3D the wonders of the corals at your feet. There is a Conservation Information Centre on Round Island, and **restaurants** on Cerf, Round and Moyenne, where writer-owner Brendon Grimshaw is buried, a grave he dug himself alongside several pirates. And promptly fell in. Initially he couldn't get out.

BEAU VALLON ★★★

A 'beautiful valley' couched between high mountains, Beau Vallon opens out onto a 6km (4-mile) bay stretching from Sunset Beach to the north all the way round to the granite cliffs of Bel Ombre, and incorporates an exquisite, mile-long scimitar beach. Shaded by huge takamaka trees, the talcum beach only 15 minutes over the mountain saddle from Victoria is the favourite with young muscled men in shades and tattoos. Golden Mile promenade here is Seychelles' playground. A dozen hotels fringe the bay, the heart of action fun: paragliding, water-skiing, scuba training and manic water Harleys are all on offer. For those less

GLIMPSES OF SEYCHELLES

Practically every vantage point in Seychelles is a 360° postcard.
• **Sans Souci pass:** a glimpse of paradise, the road out of Victoria towards Morne Seychellois National Park. A number of excellent viewpoints over the harbour, islands and town.
• **Le Niol:** if paragliding from the beach isn't your thing, this is the best view over Beau Vallon Bay.
• **Pirates Arms Hotel:** the best verandah in town for watching the laid-back life of Victoria go by.
• **Mission:** south Mahé's mountain forests, sea and sparkling coves. And further down, Thérèse and Conception islands.

NORTH MAHÉ

TAMARIND AND ZAMALAKS

Year-round there are fruits to be picked in Seychelles. You will see fallen fruit everywhere: on the roads, the mountains, and in everyone's back yard. They include:

• Tamarind. Tangy, tasty fruit, like a brown brittle peashell. Makes a lovely drink.

• Karambol. Tart star-shaped fruit. The wood makes the best roundel for tambourine-shaped *moutya* drums.

• Jackfruit. Grows on the trunk of trees. As big as a watermelon. Very rich and strong smelling.

• Red-skinned bananas. Big and fat. *Banan mil* are tiny breakfast treats. Huge *banan zak* are for cooking. There are 25 varieties of banana in Seychelles.

• Mango. The Indian king of fruits. Unripe it is made into a delicious salad with oil, vinegar, salt and pepper.

• Zamalak. White or red crispy fruits. Looks like a small apple. Good in jams and stewed.

energetic, poolside drinks are sugar-rimmed with tiny parasols and the sunsets behind Silhouette Island are, as one Cape Town visitor put it, 'to die for doll'.

The days when the Northolme Hotel would proudly advertise 24-hour electricity and 'hot baths on request' have passed. Today's paradise à la mode has to include 'infinity' pools, tennis courts, boutiques, coffee shops, dancing and water sports. Yet, for all that, even the largest hotels are hidden among the trees and you will never see more than 200 people on the beach.

One Man on a Dead Man's Chest

Near the saddle of the pass on the road from Victoria to Beau Vallon, a road twisting off to the left leads up through the granite massif and dark breadfruit forest to Le Niol, which has sweeping, lonely views of the whole Beau Vallon Bay.

Down below, at the far western end of the crescent on the Bel Ombre beach is a 50 years long treasure dig site. It's not fair that a Long John Silver haul of treasure hasn't been found in Seychelles, as every palm-laced cove and hide-away beach hints at hidden plunder, and there were certainly plenty of pirates, privateers and corsairs knocking around the islands down the years. Some of their descendants still live in Seychelles.

Grenadier Guardsman **Reginald Cruise-Wilkins** came from England to settle at Beau Vallon in 1949, determined to find the treasure of cut-throat **Olivier Le Vasseur**. *La Buse*, or the Buzzard, who ravaged the Indian Ocean in the 1770s, supposedly buried treasure worth £100 million at Bel Ombre before he felt the gallows noose tighten around his neck. He is said to have tossed a scrap of paper to the crowd on the scaffold calling, 'My treasure to the one who can under-stand'. It was this cryptogram, based partially on the labours of Hercules, that Cruise-Wilkins believed he had mastered. Working with other documents supplied by locals, and encouraged by digs that had revealed strange rock markings and the corpses of two men with earrings, he spent decades

◀ *Left: Mysterious, moody Le Niol mountain road, high above Bel Ombre (beautiful shadow) beach where a family still digs for buccaneer gold.*

and considerable amounts of money digging, constructing sea dykes and removing rock. But with the exception of a few tantalizing clues – the trigger guard of a musket, a coin of Charles I's time, the stone statue of a woman, and a cavern with a trapdoor – he died disappointed. A pirate's flag used to fly over this corner of Bel Ombre by the side of the road where Cruise-Wilkins' son, John, has not yet abandoned hope.

Off the western end of Bel Ombre there is a walking path leading into the Morne Seychellois National Park, which traverses the cliff tops to a pretty little cove called **Anse Major**, the wildest area of North Mahé.

DON'T EAT THE CRABS

Marianne North, the indomitable Victorian artist and botanist whose superb paintings of flowers and plants hang in Victoria's Natural History Museum, landed on North Mahé in 1883. She dropped her bag and screamed with wonder at the fiddler crabs 'to the amazement of my porters who said coolly they were not good to eat'.

NORTH MAHÉ AT A GLANCE

BEST TIMES TO VISIT
The cooler, drier months in Seychelles are from **Apr to Sept**. At all times of year, however, it is tropically warm and humid. It can rain at any time, but expect torrential downpours lasting several days over the **Christmas** period.

GETTING THERE
Air Seychelles flies nonstop from several hubs worldwide including Bangkok, Beijing, Dar es Salaam, Frankfurt, Johannesburg, London, Mauritius, Milan, Munich, Paris, Rome and Singapore. Other carriers link Seychelles to Doha, Dubai, Nairobi and Moscow. Air Seychelles has offices or is represented in 45 countries. Port Victoria is the sole point of entry for yachts.
Transfers: Mason's Travel and other tour operators offer transfers, or there are taxis. If you don't have much luggage, there are inexpensive and regular buses. The airport is situated some 10km (6 miles) south of Victoria.

GETTING AROUND
Hire cars are by far the most popular way to explore the island. Remember, some of the roads are precipitous. There are some 40 rental companies in Seychelles. Try Hertz at the airport, or tel: 248 4 322447, e-mail: hertz@seychelles.net
Bicycles are best hired on rural Praslin and La Digue. **Bus:** Get a timetable and map from the Central Bus Terminal, tel:

248 4 224550 or 4 280280, cnr 5th June Ave and Palm St. Destinations are digitally lit as bus approaches. Daylight (and one night circular) service only. Bus fare is SR5. **Taxis:** No meters but there is an agreed fare structure. Taxi Rank Victoria, tel: 248 4 322279. Operators' Association, tel: 248 4 323895.

WHERE TO STAY
Near Victoria
Eden Bleu, Eden Island, tel: 248 4 399100, e-mail: info@ edenbleu.com website: www. edenbleu.com Brand new downtown elegance, yacht marina and mountains. Ideal hotel (South African) for arrival in Seychelles and departures. Only shopping plaza/supermarket in Seychelles.
Bel Air Hotel, tel: 248 4 224416, e-mail: belair@seychelles. net website: www.seychelles. net/belair Cool and colonial. Overlooking Victoria; 7 rooms.
Sunrise, tel: 248 4 224560, e-mail: sunrise@intelvision.net website: www.seychelles.net/ sunrise-hotel Near Botanical Gardens; 16 rooms. Chinese cuisine and grocery shop.
La Sans Souci Guesthouse, tel: 248 4 225355, e-mail: san souci@seychelles.net website: www.seychellessecrets.com Mountain road; three rooms, restaurant, babysitting.

Beau Vallon and Surrounds
Hilton Seychelles Northolme Resort and Spa, tel: 248 4 299179, e-mail: reservations. seychelles@hilton.com

website: www.hiltonworld resorts.com 40 hill-perched rooms have jacuzzis, satellite TV and an 'infinity' pool.
Savoy Seychelles, tel: 248 4 392000, e-mail: rsvn@savoy. sc website: www.savoy.sc New large hotel (Russian) on popular Beau Vallon Bay beach. Michelin chef, champagne for breakfast.
Le Méridien Fisherman's Cove, tel: 248 4 677000, e-mail: sales.fishcove@lemeridien.com website: www.lemeridien fishermanscove.com Magnificent Sokwe music; 70 rooms.

Small Hotels
There are some 15 of these at Beau Vallon.
Daniella's Bungalows, Bel Ombre (west BVB), tel: 248 4 247914, e-mail: daniella@ seychelles.net website: www.daniellasbungalows.com Near small stream; 12 rooms.

North Circular
Manresa, N.E. Coast, tel: 248 4 241388, e-mail: manresa@ email.sc Five air-conditioned rooms; Claudette and Nicholas have run it for 20 years; restaurant.
Carana Beach Hotel, tel: 248 4 288964, e-mail: info@ caranabeach.com website: www.caranabeach.com 40 ocean front luxury suites.

Islands
There are eight resorts including Ste Anne and Cerf Island just offshore from Victoria. Try

the delightful **L'Habitation**
(12 rooms), tel: 248 4 323111,
e-mail: labicerf@seychelles.
net website: www.seychelles.
resa.com

WHERE TO EAT
Victoria
Pirates Arms, tel: 248 4
225001. Jam-packed, laid-
back, people-watching eatery.
Marie Antoinette, St Louis
Rd above Victoria, tel: 248 4
266222. Plantation House. No
guillotine but delicious Kreol
menu for past 40 years, eg
parrotfish fritters .
Le Rendez Vous, Clock Tower
roundabout, upstairs, tel: 248 4
323556. Ladies who lunch.

Beau Vallon
La Scala, Bel Ombre, tel: 248
4 247535. Superb mixed Kreol
and Italian cuisine since 1978.
Recommended.
Le Corsaire, Bel Ombre,
tel: 248 4 247171. Seaside 'yo
ho ho' and a grilled lobster.
Great atmosphere.
La Perle Noire, Beau Vallon, tel:
248 4 620220. Italian; steaks.

There are many Kreolised
restaurants, but the best Kreol
food is at:
Boathouse, Beau Vallon, tel:
248 4 247898. Sand floor.
Popular Kreol fish buffet.
Chez Gaby, Round Island
Marine Park, tel: 248 4 322111.
Lunches.
L'Habitation des Cerfs
Luxury Hotel, Cerf Island,
tel: 248 4 323111. Laid-back
beachside eating.

TOURS AND EXCURSIONS
There are many combinations
of tours and activities and
many **tour operators** including
the following:
Mason's Travel, Revolution
Ave, tel: 248 4 288888, e-mail:
info@masonstravel.com
Creole Travel Services, tel: 248
4 297000, e-mail: info@travel
services.com
7° South, Kingsgate House,
tel: 248 4 292800, e-mail:
7south@seychelles.net

Excursions
Reef Safari, tel: 248 4 288888.
This should not be missed.
A perfect day's outing.
Big Game Fishing.
Contact Marine Charter,
tel: 248 4 322126, e-mail:
mca@seychelles.net
Island Cruising. *M.V. Indian
Ocean Explorer,* seven cabins,
tel: 248 4 225844, e-mail:
info@ioexpl.com
Shamal, 50ft, three cabins,
tel: 248 4 514735, e-mail:
wworld@seychelles.net
Yacht Charter. Silhouette
Cruises. Topsail schooners,
tel: 248 4 324026, e-mail:
cruises@seychelles.net
There are many others,
particularly catamarans.
Helicopters Trips. Around
Mahé and to 10 islands, tel:
248 4 385863, e-mail:
info@helicopterseychelles.sc
Diving. There are many
options. Try Dive Seychelles,
Beau Vallon Bay Hotel,
tel: 248 4 247165.
Fly-fishing. Particularly bonefish. Contact Marine Charter

Association, near yacht club,
tel: 248 4 322126.
Bird-watching. Contact Nature
Seychelles, Roche Caiman,
tel: 248 4 601100.
Package holidays. To get the
latest good deals, visit the web
under Seychelles hotels.

USEFUL CONTACTS
Air Seychelles: tel: 248 4 384232.
Airport: tel: 248 4 381000.
Ambulance: tel: 151.
Directory Enquiries: tel: 100.
Emergency (Police and Fire):
tel: 999.
Hospital: tel: 248 4 388000.
Doctor: Dr Jivan, tel: 248 4
324008; Dr Chetty, tel: 248 4
321911.
Dentist: tel: 248 4 224852.
Pharmacy: try Berhams,
Victoria House Arcade,
tel: 248 4 225559.
Optometrist: Micock
Consulting, tel: 248 4 321177.
Tourist Information:
tel: 248 4 610800,
e-mail: info@seychelles.net
website: www.seychelles.travel
Taxis: tel: 248 4 322279.
Car Rental: Hertz (see Getting
Around) or Tropicar, tel: 248 4
373336.
Conservation: Nature
Seychelles, tel: 248 4 601100,
e-mail: nature@seychelles.net
Access to Islands: Mahé,
Praslin and La Digue are the
most accessible islands. Others
are either private, involving
special permission, or have one
resort only.

3
South and West Mahé

The southern and western areas of Mahé, caressed by the trade winds, are separated from Victoria and the main tourist areas by the island's central range of mountains. It was the last area to receive tarred roads, electricity and larger hotels, and with a myriad of hidden coves, coconut plantations and empty beaches, it is also the most rural and loveliest part of Mahé. Here you will find lone fishermen coming ashore to sell their catch of *karang* on the beach, deserted picnic coves, old plantation houses sleeping among the *zak* fruit and banana trees, people walking barefoot in the tiny villages, and old men on their way to the local store carrying palm-frond shopping bags. As always, the high, jungle-covered mountains brood above, offering cool, airy walks with wide views of hillside, reef and sparkling sea, while in the forests of Morne Seychellois National Park survives a living museum of unique and unusual plants and creatures.

CENTRAL MAHÉ AND THE MOUNTAINS

The mountains of Mahé fall down to the sea in a riot of tropical greenery and dramatic black precipices. Rising abruptly out of the ocean, the mountains are almost constantly shrouded in swirling mist and flecked by bright sunlight, creating the dappled, eerie atmosphere of true montane forest, the hidden home of rare and exotic plants.

Morne Seychellois National Park covers about 30km² (12 sq miles), incorporating the highest of Mahé's misty peaks and a large section of the western interior. The

◄ *Opposite: Majestic granite mountains in Morne Seychellois National Park.*

SOUTH AND WEST MAHÉ

Don't Miss

★★★ **Walks in the mountains**, especially the exotic misty mountain walk known as Casse Dent (teeth-breaker) in the lea of Morne Seychellois, the highest mountain. The trail starts uphill from the tea factory.

★★★ **Grand'Anse Beach**: long, wild and beautiful.

★★ **Snorkelling** in Port Launay Marine Park.

★★ **The chance to go exploring**: 'grab-a-picnic-find-a-cove'.

★★ **Domaine de Val des Pres Heritage Plantation House and Craft Village**, Anse aux Pins: artists at work.

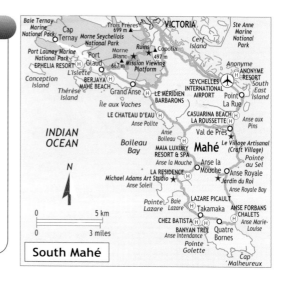

South Mahé

Mountain Bird

The *payanke* (literally *paille en queue* – old straw tail), the white-tailed tropicbird, has two feathers that flow out 30cm (1ft) behind its large, white, streamlined body. They are sea birds whose preferred delicacies are squid or flying fish. Often seen in pairs, especially during the stiff-winged courtship flight (when the noise they make sounds almost like sneezing), they prefer to fish far out to sea. A quick and powerful flyer, the tropicbird seems to symbolize the space, freedom and beauty of all that is Seychelles.

highest point is the mountain **Morne Seychellois** itself, at 905m (2970ft). There are no settlements and only one road through the park; it is all mountainous jungle, towering trees and mysterious nature. From Victoria, the **Sans Souci** mountain road over to Port Glaud cuts through the park, winding up the hillside and offering stunning views over the harbour and multi-pastel reef platforms below. It passes a number of interesting buildings, such as the American Embassy in a house called '1776', where Archbishop Makarios of Cyprus lived during his exile.

As the often precipitous road twists its way under the towering peaks, it passes the starting points for sign-posted walking trails which lead into the park and up to the peaks of **Trois Frères, Copolia** and **Morne Blanc** respectively.

At **Mission** there is a platform with spectacular views over the western coast, while on the descent into Port Glaud the **Tea Tavern** is a good place to sample and buy six different tea flavours including *citronelle* and cinnamon.

Morne Seychellois National Park

The park contains the best of the remaining indigenous forest of Seychelles, the giant lowland trees having been cut long ago, mainly to fuel cinnamon factories. There is something haunting and silently magnificent about the vast gothic cathedral of the forest. The canopy of trees soars 12m (39ft) above you as you walk, and all around green light plays on the **lichens, ferns,** straggling **creepers** and **old man's beard**. The best way to see the park beyond the road is to walk up one of the signposted paths. (Buy a trail map at Antigone in Victoria.) But it is advisable to go with an experienced guide. Be careful of deep cracks between boulders which are often hidden by the carpet of damp leaves, and sharp high drops often ending in swamps. There are nine trails in the national park.

Nearly all of the 70 or so endemic flowering plants and trees of Seychelles are found somewhere in the National Park: **screw pines, palms,** *koko maron* (the coconut tree named after a runaway slave), **orchids** and the **pitcher plant**. It is highly likely that Morne Seychellois is home to the total world population of both the ***bwa-d-fer*** (ironwood) and the jellyfish tree, ***bwa mediz***. This tree, which was sensationally rediscovered by botanists in 1970, is about 8m (26ft) high with tiny, rose-like flowers which become clusters of sunburnt fruit like upside-down parachutes, hence the name jellyfish. There are only about 11 trees

MISSION

Just below the crest of the Forêt Noir (Black Forest) pass on the Sans Souci road there is a viewing platform overlooking tea and coffee plantations, called Mission. A hundred and fifty years ago it was a school, Venn's Town, for the children of the 2409 Africans rescued from Arab slavers by the 'gallantry of the British navy'. A modern echo: two Somali pirate ships were sunk by Seychelles naval gunboats when they refused to surrender. Restored and historically trail-mapped, an avenue of trees divides the deserted moss-covered ruins from the hush of the flanking forest. It is a gracious, quiet spot, with the sound of streams in the valley below, bees, and the pleasant scent of *citronelle* grass in the wind.

▼ *Below: Hideaway houses in the mountains.*

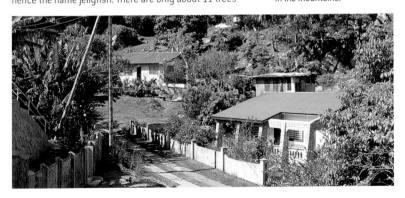

still growing in the wild, so rare they merit their own genus grouping.

Apart from the endemics, there are a lot of what botanists call exotics, not because they are spectacularly colourful, but because they are strangers. One example is the pale, grey-trunked **albizia** tree, which is common in Africa; another is the **cinnamon** bush, whose leaves exude a sweet tangy smell when you crumple it in your hand.

Frogs such as the **pygmy piping frog**, which makes a lot of noise considering that it is only the size of a cowrie shell, are found in the wet uplands, and seven of Seychelles' unique birds make use of the high green canopy. You might spot the **Seychelles kestrel**, or the **bare-legged scops owl**, while the noisy **Seychelles bulbul** plays the same warning role as the African 'Go Away' bird.

Grand'Anse

Grand'Anse, on the west coast over the La Misère road, is a long curve of wave-lashed beach which is often completely deserted; in some ways it is even more attractive than Beau Vallon. Watched over by giant *takamaka* trees, its waters lie open to the wind and ocean without the barrier of reef common to many of Mahé's beaches. The dangerous ocean currents running off the beach claimed the life of Governor John Thorpe in 1961 as he was trying to rescue a child.

▶ *Opposite: A clutch of yellowhusk drinking coconuts.*
▼ *Below: Grand'Anse beach is beautiful, but occasionally swept by dangerous currents.*

During the southeast monsoon winds it is Seychelles' surfing beach.

There are less than 1000ha (2470 acres) of arable land in Seychelles. **The Ministry of Agriculture Research Station** farm at Grand'Anse specializes in researching a wide range of tropical fruits, with a view to increasing yields in the islands. Behind the strip of fertile land the mountains rise steeply into the Morne Seychellois National Park. This particular area is known as Grand Bois, which is believed to be a good place to find the elusive jellyfish tree, although you would need a guide to do so.

The aerials at the T-junction of the coastal road with the **La Misère** road belong to the BBC World Service Relay Station. Look out for the signs. Head northwest, and you will pass Grand'Anse

and reach **Port Glaud** and the **Sans Souci** road. Beyond this on the coast are the marine national parks at **Port Launay** and **Baie Ternay**, where hawksbill turtles breed, and the green-backed heron, or *makak* in Kreol, is often spotted. Port Launay's expanse of palms and silent paths mark the abandoned and crumbling Seychelles National Youth Service Camp, scheduled to be an exclusive Emirates Airlines resort at some stage.

Standing off the coast at this point are the two substantial islands of **Thérèse** and **Conception**. The islands lie opposite the derelict Mahé Beach hotel which had only a man-made beach and had to make one from scratch. In front of Thérèse, the tiny **L'Islette** is a delightful spot sitting in the middle of the cove where the Mare aux Cochons river emerges. The *Zwazo Banann* or *Linet* (White Eye) is a LBJ (Little Brown Job) and critically endangered. The world's last remaining 300 are found on Conception, with 31 successfully transferred to Frégate.

WEDDING IN PARADISE

Islands of love, Garden of Eden, frangipanis and whispering palms. It all started in the 1970's on romance-bedazzled Bird Island. Couples book a civil wedding package and are married barefoot in the surf at sunset. Now many tour operators and large hotels offer the same. Book four months in advance, and bring all legal certificates. Church weddings can also be arranged but involve a bit more groundwork, and have to be in addition to the civil ceremony. You have to live in Seychelles for a minimum of three days before the wedding. Unlike Las Vegas – but then marriage is more of a gamble there.

SOUTH AND WEST MAHÉ

Barbarons

Barbarons is a low-lying plateau south of Grand'Anse which rises gradually from the coast through lush coconut plantations to a height of 600m (1970ft). Reef and rock lie close inshore with a wild and beautiful beach, somewhat obscured by a multi-room yellow-roofed resort, **Le Méridien Barbarons**. A little further is the **Chateau d'Eau**, a delightfully elegant French plantation house and small hotel.

Nearby there used to be an orchid nursery. Very appropriate for Seychelles where they grow luxuriantly, with some 25 local varieties, many of which are endemic, including the national flower. Unfortunately the farm has closed down.

THE SOUTH

Hidden coves with steep, twisty roads leading to them are a feature of South Mahé, and there always seems to be a charming little village behind these hidden gems. Some of the beaches are less than 50m (55yd) long and usually backed by heavy stands of *takamaka* trees leaning over the waters. It is in the south that the last *moutyas* were danced, *kasye* fishing traps lean up against trees, spoken English is more unusual, and domino players will gather in noisy groups in the villages. To this day folk from Anse Soleil or Quatre Bornes are regarded by the sophisticates of Victoria as coming from the sticks.

Anse Boileau

For many years it was thought that Lazare Picault, the first Frenchman to land in Seychelles, had done so in the bay named after him in South Mahé, where the Plantation Club is now owned by a Middle Eastern sheikh. (So they say.)

ORCHIDS

Worldwide there are 17,000 species of orchid. Seychelles is home to 25, most of them epiphitic, meaning that they grow on other plants.

• Wild *payanke* or tropicbird orchid, the national flower.

• Wild vanilla orchid: large white flowers with an orange peach centre that bloom after rain and die by noon. There is no vanilla in them.

• Orchid tree: pink and mauve flowers. The seeds of some varietals are occasionally used for coffee.

• Phaius, or ground forest orchid, with leaves over 30cm (1ft) in length.

• Cultivated vanilla: pale green flowers and thick leaves on vines zigzagging up stakes. Big business in Seychelles 100 years ago, deforested slopes are witness to its popularity. Today it largely grows wild on trees.

In fact, Picault came ashore in the much more practical – for anchoring both sailing ship and beach-bound longboat – Boileau Bay, slightly further north. An ancient anchor above the beach serves as a memorial of his arrival.

A drive along the length of the bay leads past spindly coconut trees to the handsome, 160-year-old church of **Notre Dame de Sept Douleurs** (Our Lady of Seven Sorrows), which has some magnificent hardwood marquetry covering both the high ceiling and its support columns in mottled, chevron zigzag patterns. The altar crucifixion tableau is as gory as any pious 19th-century self-flagellating artist could devise.

From the shallow tidal waters of Anse Boileau beach, the coastal mountains stretch left and right like enveloping bird wings, in a lush panorama that prompted Picault to name Mahé the 'Isle of Abundance'. Part of the forest by the **Montagne Posée** mountain road is still known as L'Abondance. There is a trail which starts by the Cable and Wireless Station near **Bon Espoir** at the top of the pass and leads to a summit of 501m (1644ft). Anse Boileau's hinter-

---

MOUNTAIN ROADS

There are six main passes over the mountains and many unmarked narrow ones. Just turn up any concrete road and explore. The smaller the mountain road, the more old, rural Seychelles.

• **Sans Souci:** from Victoria through Morne Seychellois National Park.
• **La Misère:** Plaisance to Grand'Anse.
• **Montagne Posée:** from Anse aux Pins
• **Les Canelles:** from Anse Royale to Anse La Mouche. Stop at Le Jardin du Roi.
• **Quatre Bornes:** Banyan Tree road. Fruit and roadside barbecues.
• **Adventure tip:** turn right at the yellow shop 1.6km (1 mile) south of Anse Royale Church through Val d'Endor. Comes out at Harvey's store.

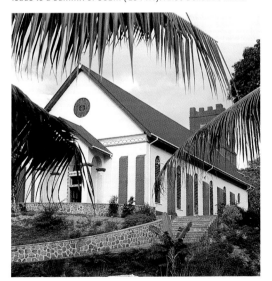

◀◀ *Opposite: Thérèse and Conception Islands seen from above Port Glaud.*
◀ *Left: Intricate multi-wood marquetry decorates the secret interior of the lovely Church of the Seven Sorrows at Anse Boileau.*

▲ *Above: Facing Souris or Mouse Island, a favourite cove for families.*

FORESTS OF THE SEA

Care to do the Mangrove Board Walk? No, it's not a dance but a man-made deck in the mangrove wildlife wetlands near Grand'Anse, Mahé. From the view platform you can spy crabs, fish and breeding birds. The stilt-like roots of mangroves march forth in the mud throwing out shoots, reclaiming land. Mangrove, *mangliye* in Kreol, comes from a Bahamas-Indian word. Mangroves provide a red floor polish. Aldabra's vastness of mangroves are nesting perches for boobies who seldom evade frigate birds stealth-bomb diving to frighten them out of fish catches. Denude shores of mud-gripping mangroves to build yacht marinas, and tsunamis become more destructive.

land is agricultural with an (now closed) orchid nursery, and further south the lovely Barbarons Botanical Gardens recently upgraded to a Biodiversity Centre. At Anse La Mouche, stop for a meal at **La Sirene** or **Anchor Café**. Ask for fish or any Seychelles fish curry. They are all tasty.

Corsair Country

In the hook of **Anse la Mouche**, there is a magnificent panorama of the whole of west Mahé – a great long tumble of mountain, cloud and sea. Other than the lofty perch of Mission in the hills there is probably no grander view on Mahé. Perhaps it is the reason why the Hodoul family settled in this area generations ago.

Mention the name of sea captain **Jean François Hodoul** to an old Seychellois and you'll probably notice a faint shiver. An adventurer and successful privateer, 'Le Corsair' was also a man of refined and sophisticated tastes, reputed to have the best table in Seychelles. A tiny island in Victoria's yacht basin and a smidgen of Aldabra atoll are named Hodoul. A local almanac of 1819 records that Hodoul '... ravaged the Red Sea, Gulf of Persia, Malabar and Coromandel Coasts, Sumatra and Java', yet Seychelles was always his base. He settled down to run his estates initially in Silhouette, then Beau Vallon, before moving to Mamelles, just south of Victoria, where his great mansion still stands.

His descendants feature regularly in the history of the islands and in politics. The family house at Anse la Mouche is near 'La Residence' holiday villas, built by Marie-Anne Hodoul, the great-granddaughter of the corsair.

This area of the south coast used to have several old plantation houses. These venerable gems are fast decaying or disappearing in Seychelles – a great loss. Coral raised verandahs, rusty tin roofs and big wooden exteriors are hidden from the beach among flowers and thick greenery. If you are not a beach person, wander from cove to cove, spot one of the old beauties, abandoned, shutters closed and ravaged by salt winds. One of the charms of these houses, particularly on La Digue, was that almost every one was a living museum with a treasure trove of historical artefacts. British civil servants were fond of denigrating the planters, but in an agriculturally hostile environment it was always a struggle to introduce and sustain new crops, plants and animals. They did, however, have paw-paws, coconuts, breadfruit, spices, tamarinds and their stern God to sustain them. And the sort of views you get at Anse la Mouche.

PLANTATION HOUSES

Some of the unusual features that you can still find in Seychelles plantation houses:
• Sweeping steps up to the verandah made of coral.
• Flower displays atop a polished trunk of coco de mer.
• Wide rattan lounge chairs with crocheted antimacassars.
• *Garde manger:* a wire-meshed box hanging in the kitchen from the roof to deter rats, with a cone of water suspended around the cord to combat ants.
• *Grenier:* granary in the loft. Separate window entrance to winch up maize, rice or coffee.
• *Gargoulet:* water jug.
• *Boulwar:* iron kettle.

▼ Below: A hidden mountain cottage, but with today's vital accessory, a TV antenna.

SOUTH AND WEST MAHÉ

The Southern Tip

As the road turns out of Anse la Mouche over to **Baie Lazare**, you will find the studio of famous Seychelles artist Michael Adams overlooking **Anse aux Poules Bleues**. A little further on there is a broken road which leads to **Anse Soleil**'s tiny, sunset-shimmering beach. There used to be an old sugar cane mill in the forest. Now there is a small hotel and tiny café.

After Takamaka, just off the road before Quatre Bornes village, there is a handsome 115-year-old plantation house, the only thatched double-storey one still standing in Seychelles, the rest having adopted corrugated iron decades ago.

At the top of the saddle the road comes to **Quatre Bornes**, or four milestone village, with its brightly coloured shops hanging over the road. (Try the *moutay*, a *koeksister*-like honey snack.) Visit any of these little southern villages on a Sunday and you'll see the scenes of old-fashioned, rural Mahé: football games in the dusty road, quartets of hand-slapping domino players beneath the mango trees, neighbours sitting and chatting by their front porch, and washing laid out on the grass to dry.

From Quatre Bornes a narrow, twisting road leads to what

◄ *Left: Mangrove wetland rich in small wildlife, near Grand'Anse.*
◄◄ *Opposite: The only thatched double-storey plantation house still standing, after 115 years, in Seychelles.*

used to be called Southern Seas, a 101ha (250-acre) wild and windswept wilderness garden at Petite Boileau. This is Seychelles, its birds, trees, butterflies and solitude as it was 50 years ago. For some reason it's closed. Does a billionaire marina developer have his pirate spyglass on it? Beware: the lonely reef-free bays are not protected from the shifting currents that sweep around this wild coast, where turtles nest, land's end of Mahé.

Jardin du Roi

In 1772, **Pierre Poivre** (Peter Pepper), administrator of Île-de-France (the French name for the earlier Dutch Mauritius), picked an expedition to go to Seychelles to develop a spice nursery. He believed that conditions on Mahé might allow the crops to compete with the Dutch spices monopoly in the East. Especially pepper, vital for preserving meat in Europe's winter.

The spot chosen for the garden was on a broad, low-lying plain of rich black soil well watered by two rivers, just up from the longest beach on the island called **Anse Royale**, in the southeast of Mahé. The nursery developed gradually, first rivalling the earlier, private venture at the settlement on Ste Anne's Island, and eventually replacing it. Within eight years they had cultivated cloves, nutmeg and pepper brought in from the Moluccas in Indonesia, and cinnamon from Ceylon. The nursery was deliberately burnt

---

UP THE AIRY MOUNTAIN

Please check (eg with Mason's Travel, Antigone bookshop or your local tour operator) all pictogram-marked mountain walks before starting out, and ask for the relevant maps.

• **Glacis Trois Frères.**
In Morne Seychellois National Park, a trail to the top of Trois Frères (699m; 2293ft), the second-highest massif on the island. Start near Sans Souci Forestry Station. Spectacular views, but beware of cloud and do not stray from path.
4–5 hours.

• **Casse Dent.** Near Mission through Forêt Noire passing Morne Seychellois.

• **Morne Blanc** (667m; 2188ft). Start a little further down, nearer the Tea Factory. Morne Blanc cliff drops 250m (820ft).
4–5 hours.

• **Copolia.** Eastern side of Sans Souci road, past the forest station. Up to a height of 497m (1631ft). 3 hours.

• **Summit of Mt Brulée** between Anse Boileau and Anse aux Pins.

• **Bel Ombre** coast to Anse Major.

▲ *Above: Jardin du Roi's plantation house museum (and cinnamon ices), a favourite with school kids.*

CINNAMON

Cinnamon (an old Hebrew word) grows wild all over Seychelles. The spice was introduced at the Jardin du Roi on Mahé in 1772 and, of all the spice trees, has proved to be the most successful. Economically insignificant today, 40 years ago it provided 30% of Seychelles' foreign currency. Use it on pancakes, in jams, stews, or pluck a leaf and suck it as a pick-me-up. Buy bark rolls or quills in the market. In days past a brown-stained stream flowing down a beach meant distillation.

to the ground in 1780 when the farmers were told a British ship was sailing into Port Royale (Victoria) harbour, as the secrets of the spices were too valuable to fall into the enemy's hands. The man o' war turned out to be French.

In 1994, three young Seychellois with a sense of history opened their own Jardin du Roi at Anse Royale. Run by Micheline Georges, whose family has farmed this area since 1854 (with a special stamp for each vanilla pod), the gardens of 32ha (79 acres) are planted not only with the original spices but such modern additions as cardamom and the 19th-century money-spinner patchouli. It is a great spot to wander among the scented trees and flowers. Sunday lunch in the creperie is tops, especially the home-made spices ice cream. You'll see the old plantation house, museum, spices shop and reptile house. From the hill above the garden, Roche Gratte Fesse (literally 'scratch your bum rock'), there are splendid views of Anse Royale's beach, village and the towers of the two churches built right on the beach, one Anglican in 1889 by Englishman William Green, first private owner of the Jardin du Roi and great-great-grandfather of Micheline Georges, and the other Catholic, St Joseph's, in 1854.

Anse aux Pins

Just around the corner from the airport, Anse aux Pins is a busy, crowded village and the home of the Reef, Seychelles' first big tourist hotel, now almost abandoned. Close-in reef stretches past the village to the casuarina-tufted **Pointe au Sel**, 6km (3.5 miles) distant. The rumble of the breakers can be heard night and day, as the thin, pine-like *filão* that give the beach its name fret in the trades – although the trees aren't in fact true pines at all.

Being close to the airport, this bay is often the last view visitors have of Seychelles, as their jet gains altitude above the emerald sea. Fifty years ago, there were only eight – all rustic – hotels in Seychelles. Now there are over 200. Three of the original ones, Pirates Arms, Sunset and Northolme, are still functioning. Anse Aux Pins, being near the airport, saw the first tourist-boom hotels. Eleven still flourish there. There is a nine-hole golf course here, the only one on Mahé.

La Marine, where replicas of old French sailing boats are carved, as they are at Domaine de Val des Pres, a fascinating plantation house museum, shouldn't be missed. The **Kreol Instititi** for furthering the language and culture of Seychelles is housed in an old plantation house called Maison St Joseph halfway down the bay. The beach is not the best as the reef is too close – although it can be good for finding octopus.

ON THE MOVE

There are some 500km (311 miles) of surfaced roads in Seychelles, and some 11,000 motor vehicles of which 300 are taxis, 1100 self-drive and 200 buses, the main form of transport. The days of rickshas, *pousse*, have long passed, as have the flat-bottomed pirogue canoes that waited 'for madam' like carriages in the shallows at dinner parties. Now the waters are graced by catamarans, the occasional helicopter shuttle above and Toyota 4x4's on the double highway to the airport.

▼ *Below: Spiritual solitude in the lea of Anse Royale's twice renovated church.*

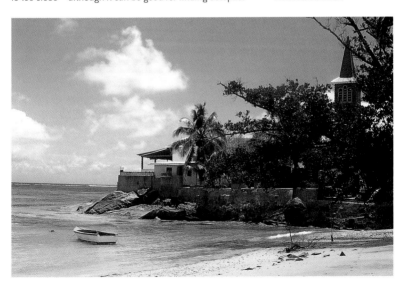

SOUTH AND WEST MAHÉ AT A GLANCE

For further information see also North Mahé at a Glance (pp54–55)

For further information see also North Mahé at a Glance (pp54–55)

BEST TIMES TO VISIT

It rains heavily in **Dec, Jan** and **Feb,** while the southeast trade winds from **Apr** to **Oct** bring refreshing breezes to all but the northwest of the island. Temperature stays at a steady 27ºC (81ºF) all year, with a tropical humidity of 80–85%. Many hotels have air conditioning; others, cool fans and large shuttered windows.

GETTING THERE

Other than cruise ships or your own yacht, the only way to get to Mahé is to **fly**. There are scheduled services from Africa (Johannesburg and Nairobi), Europe, and the Middle and Far East. The international airport is on the east coast of Mahé, a 15-minute drive from Victoria. Airport **transfers** are usually arranged by your hotel or tour operator.

GETTING AROUND

Car hire is the favourite for touring the rural areas of Mahé. There are practically no gravel roads left, and plenty of passes over the mountains which are steep, winding roads with marvellous views of forest and shore below. Beware of steep drops off the narrow roads, and tight corners. The speed limit is 65kph (40kph in towns and villages). There are not many petrol stations. Make sure you fill up or you'll pay a premium. Hire cars usually come with an empty tank.

Taxis are available in Victoria,

the airport, and at the larger hotels; 24-hour service. Note that taxi fares are relatively expensive. One of the best ways to get around is on the local **buses**. The service is cheap and regular but they don't operate after 19:00. A **regular bus service** is available around the beaches and villages of South Mahé and over the mountains. Call out *'devan'* ('up ahead') when you want to disembark.

WHERE TO STAY

Large hotels. Usually best beaches. Spas, tennis, kiddies corners, massage, wellness and all *zatt jazz*.

Four Seasons Resort Petite Anse, tel: 248 4 393000, e-mail: res.seychelles@four seasons.com website: www. fourseasons.com 80 villas.

Maia Luxury Resort, Anse Louis, tel: 248 4 390000, e-mail: res ervations@southernsun.sc website: www.maia.com.sc Spa, 30 rooms, 300 species of garden plants.

Banyan Tree, Intendance, tel: 248 4 383500, e-mail: reservations-seychelles@ banyantree.com website: www. banyantree.com 47 villas, costing up to US$4500 per villa. Each villa has its own pool, jacuzzi and steam room.

Small and Budget Hotels

Note: The smaller the hotel, the better it tends to be.

Lazare Picault, Anse Gaulettes, tel: 248 4 361111, e-mail:

lazarpco@seychelles.net website: www.lazarepicault hotel.com Sea views, 14 chalets.

Surfers, Anse Parnel, tel: 248 4 371100, e-mail: surfersbeach@ seychelles.net website: www. surfersbeach.net Self-catering. Six lovely bungalows.

La Residence, Anse La Mouche, tel: 248 4 371733, e-mail: villa@ seychelles.net Three villas, five studios.

Crown Beach, Pointe Au Sel, tel: 248 4 382800, e-mail: alice@ crownbeachseychelles.com website: www.crownbeach seychelles.com Cricket pitch-sized beds. 12 suites.

Chalets d'Anse Forbans, tel: 248 4 366111, e-mail: info@ forbans.com website: www. forbans.com 14 self-catering beach chalets.

Le Chateau d'Eau, Barbarons, tel: 248 4 378177, fax: 248 4 378388. Five rooms, plantation elegance.

Hotel La Roussette, Anse aux Pins, tel: 248 4 376245, e-mail: manager@hotel-larousette.com www.Hotel-LaRoussette.com 5 bungalows.

Pied Dans L'eau, Anse Royale, tel: 248 4 430110, e-mail: piedanslo@intelvision.net website: www.piedansleau.sc Six luxury self-catering apartments.

WHERE TO EAT

Carefree, Anse aux Pins, tel: 248 4 375237. First small hotel in Seychelles (built in 1971). Run by Zita and Leon Monthy. Kreol cuisine.

For further information see also North Mahé at a Glance (pp54–55)

Surfers Beach Restaurant, tel: 248 4 371100. Sunday lunch favourite.

Chez Batista's, Takamaka Beach, tel: 248 4 366300. Seats 200.

Vye Marmit, Pomme Cannelle, Au Cap, East Coast, tel: 248 4 376155. In Val des Près craft village. Set menu, almost forgotten Kreol dishes. Recommended.

Kaz Kreol Pizzeria, Anse Royale Beach, tel: 248 4 371680. Closed Mondays.

Le Reduit, Takamaka, tel: 248 4 366116. Laid-back beach curries, great views.

La Sirene, Anse Poules Bleues, tel: 248 4 361339. Lunches only. Near Michael Adams' art studio overlooking Anse La Mouche.

Chez Plume, Anse Boileau, tel: 248 4 355050. Tasty Kreol specialities served here.

Les Dauphins Heureux, Anse Royale, tel: 248 4 430100. Elegant seashore dining.

What to Eat

A good bet is octopus curry, and also fruit bat paté, raw mango salad, palmis, breadfruit in coconut milk, grilled *kordonnyen*, or *tectec* soup. Try the bananas in syrup.

Tours and Excursions

Bird-watching. Contact Nature Seychelles, Birdlife International, tel: 248 4 601100. Buy Adrian Skerrett's books. Incidentally, the noisy whistler is the Indian mynah.

Golf. Reef, Anse aux Pins,

tel: 248 4 376234.

Walking Trails. Contact the Tourist Office in Independence House, Victoria for trail maps of Morne Seychellois National Park, or Antigone Bookshop, Victoria House Arcade, tel: 248 4 225443, or any tour operator.

Diving. Any local large hotel, or Island Ventures Dive Seychelles PADI 5★, Beau Vallon Bay Hotel, tel: 248 4 345445. There are 10 good dive sites off West Mahé including Baie Ternay Marine Park.

Dancing. The larger hotels feature sega music and dancing displays, usually at weekends.

Tennis. Large hotels.

Fishing. Contact Marine Charter, tel: 248 4 322126. Small beach fishermen may take you out in their boat.

Helicopter Scenic Trips. For a great view of paradise, tel: 248 4 385863. There are ten helipads in Seychelles.

Reef Exploring. Wear a pair of tough shoes and wade or swim to the reef at low tide, or go by boat. Don't snorkel alone, never collect live shells or coral, and be wary of spiky black sea urchins.

Swimming. Seychellois tend to overplay swimming dangers. But be wary at

Intendance, Anse Takamaka and Grand'Anse. During May–October there are strong currents, waves and winds.

Useful Contacts

Air Seychelles (Airport): tel: 248 4 391010.

Ambulance: tel: 151.

Directory Enquiries: tel: 100.

Emergency (Police and Fire): tel: 999.

Doctor: Dr Jivan, tel: 248 4 324008; Dr Chetty, tel: 248 4 321911.

Dentist: tel: 248 4 224852.

Pharmacy: Berhams, Victoria House Arcade, tel: 248 4 225559.

Optometrist: Micock Consulting, tel: 248 4 321177.

Tourist Information: tel: 248 4 610800, e-mail: info@ seychelles.net, website: www. seychelles.travel

Taxis: tel: 248 4 322279.

Car Rental: Palm Cars, tel: 248 4 712102, Hertz, tel: 248 4 322447, www.seychelles.net/ hertz

Access to Islands: Cerf, La Digue, Mahé and Praslin are the main public islands, 14 others are private. They and others involve special permissions.

GRAND'ANSE	J	F	M	A	M	J	J	A	S	O	N	D
AVERAGE TEMP. °F	81	82	82	82	82	81	79	79	79	81	81	79
AVERAGE TEMP. °C	27	27.5	28	28	28	27	26	26	26.5	27	27	26.5
SEA TEMP. °F	82	80	82	80	78	77	73	73	73	79	77	80
SEA TEMP. °C	28	27	28	27	26	25	23	23	23	26	25	27
RAINFALL in	17	7	25	7	9	6	5	7	7	9	9	11
RAINFALL mm	422	180	237	175	233	146	130	170	169	225	233	274
Days of Rainfall	11	6	7	6	8	6	6	6	7	6	8	10

4
Praslin

For many people, the island of Praslin is the real Seychelles. A rural, languid island of beaches, palms, and country roads, it has all the ingredients of the Garden of Eden image that made Seychelles famous. High in the hills, the **Vallée de Mai** is home to the 100ft tall coco de mer palms that bear the largest fruit in the world. Theories have suggested that the giant palms are the biblical trees of Adam and Eve, and the valley the paradise that man was heir to before being tempted into mortality.

Sited 40km (25 miles) east of Mahé, Praslin is the archipelago's second largest island, 11km (7 miles) long and 4km (2.5 miles) wide. It is the choice holiday spot of Seychellois themselves, and visitors who have discovered it tend not to linger too long at Mahé airport as they transfer to one of the small Otter aircraft that make the 15-minute hop across the ocean.

Praslin's highest peak, at 367m (1204ft), is only a third that of Morne Seychellois on Mahé, and its population is just over 9000 people. There are no towns, and only two villages, at **Grand'Anse** and **Baie Ste Anne** where the old-fashioned schooners tie up. But even in these quaint settlements you never get the impression of there being many people around, for Praslin is laid-back, relaxed and unspoilt in every way. The pace of life encourages you to explore on foot, to a distant beach, up the trails in the hills, or simply along to a lone corner shop on the Anse Kerlan road. You may well meet one of the eccentric and interesting artists, writers

◄ *Opposite: Cool crystal waters, Praslin.*

73

PRASLIN

DON'T MISS

★★★ **Vallée de Mai**, home of the coco de mer fruit and palms. World Heritage Site. Trails and curio shop.
★★★ **Fond Ferdinand Reserve**, Anse Marie-Louise. Take the 2km forest trail. Seychelles Heritage Foundation.
★★★ **Côte d'Or**. Beach of boutiques, boats, self-catering villas, Rita's Art Gallery.
★★ **Bicycle ride** around the mainly flat circular road from Côte d'Or to Baie Ste Anne, Consolation, Grand'Anse and Anse Kerlan.
★★ **Dive or snorkel** in the Marine Park in Curieuse Bay.
★★ Look out for **Seychelles Heritage Foundation/Raffles** roadsigns.
★ Walk to **Anse Volbert** or **Baie Chevalier**.

and bohemians the island seems to attract, and come to understand the depth of affection in an old island song. 'Praslin, *mon* Praslin,' it goes, 'I will never let you go'.

The economy of Praslin was founded for many years on coconut, vanilla and patchouli plantations, fishing, and quarrying (Praslin's red granite is prized for building façades on Mahé), but increasingly the island has set its foundations in tourism. Originally keen to maintain the number of hotels on Praslin at an ecologically sustainable level, Praslin has naturally succumbed to the siren lure of development. Raffles (think Singapore) Resort is the latest.

AROUND PRASLIN
Grand'Anse

Grand'Anse is and always has been the bohemian backwater of Seychelles. It is on the western side of Praslin, but remains exposed to the trade winds that come thrashing through the palms, with waves tearing endlessly at the long line of reef far out to sea. The first hotel on Praslin, known as Grand'Anse Ideal Home, was followed by a thatched two-roomed bungalow used by the visiting Mahé doctor on his rounds of the islands. The latter is still there

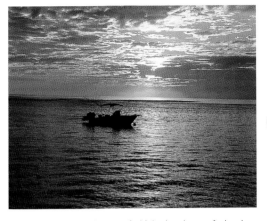

◀ *Left: Solitary fishing boat captured in the sunset at Grand'Anse.*

after 40 years, though now refurbished and part of a lovely series of luxury duplex chalets on the beach called Indian Ocean Lodge. In the early days it was given the glamorous name of Mickey Mouse – and one of the guests over the years was another Hollywood star, Ronald Reagan.

With a dozen establishments such as Beach Villa, the venerable Britannia, little Indian shops and a host of self-catering villas, the village seems almost deliberately to cultivate a rakish bottle-of-rum ambience. Apart from the smart Barclays Bank, lovely library and Post Office, many of the colourfully painted tin-roofed buildings look as if they might fall over at any moment. There's a fish market, Nadia's Internet Café, and Murugan's Trading Store (both in Ocean Plaza building). Peaking over the palms is the steeple of **St Matthew the Apostle**, a church dedicated in 1859, while the coco de mer-crested independence monument is a favourite place to stop, chat and have a beer.

Grand'Anse is not a good swimming beach by Seychelles' superlative standards (**beware sandflies**), but the long seaweed-strewn stretch of sand is a favourite with beach-combers. Between the sea and the hills a wide plain with coconut trees wafts back from the narrow road that hides the occasional house and the handsome bell tower of **St Joseph's** (1854) church.

PRASLIN

▲ *Above: Yachts, ferries and occasionally an inter-island cruise ship at Baie Ste Anne's jetty anchorage.*
▶ *Opposite: Anse La Blague (Cove of Tricks), south Praslin, where yours may be the only stranger's footprints on the shore.*

Baie Ste Anne

Just behind Grand'Anse stands the central ridge of Praslin's hills with their distinctive patches of red granite soil. The mountains were once covered in huge forests but sadly fire ravaged them long ago. The main road of the island climbs through the hills, passing the entrance to the Vallée de Mai near the summit, before descending towards the sweeping curve of Baie Ste Anne.

Baie Ste Anne is the capital of Praslin, if such an expression can be justified by this sleepy seaside village, with its little cluster of small shops, school, hospital and power plant. On the beachfront you might still see men climbing the coconut trees to extract *kalou* toddy. The spider-scramble up the trees that young men used to perform is rare these days, so look out for the trees with ladders leaning against them.

The village has always been a wooden boat-building centre and is the landing stage for yachts sailing the 'Big Indy' ocean around the many islands of Seychelles and the fast Cat Cocos ferry that plies between Mahé and Praslin. There are few of the old schooners left today which, with creaking booms and tight sails, are great fun. Baie Ste Anne, like Mahé's eastern flank, has had to suffer the indignity of reclamation off its sea wall but arriving at Baie Ste Anne from the sea is always a lovely sight, with the wide sweep of the sparkling bay, the fishing boats anchored, and the green rise up to the mysterious forest behind.

Go Local

Where is this bus going?	*Kote sa bis pe ale?*
Are you going to the Vallée de Mai?	*Ou pe al Val di Me?*
Is this our boat for La Digue?	*Sa nou bato pou La Digue?*
Is Anse Kerlan far?	*I lwen Anse Kerlan?*
Can you play moutya?	*Ou konn zwe moutya?*
What is this beach called?	*Kimanyer sa lans i apele?*
What is this fish called?	*Kimanyer sa pwason i apele?*

Côte d'Or

Côte d'Or along the shores of Anse Volbert bay is a 4km (2½-mile) expanse of soft white sand fringed with palms and yellow sea hibiscus. These flowers have a deep purple centre which turns orange by afternoon. Côte d'Or has a string of hotels, **Tante Mimi's Casino** (Salon Privé, chemmy, slots) and umpteen small hotels and holiday activities along 'the strip' including windsurfing, sailing, diving and snorkelling trips to nearby **Curieuse Island Marine Park**. You can even explore the depths on a night dive if you would like to see spiny red, and huge crayfish – which normally hide in their coral caves – spidering along. Tiny and thickly wooded Chauvre Souris (Fruit Bat Island), sits Cinderella-pert and pretty 500m off the beach.

Hidden from the larger hotels is the **Café des Arts**, and along the main road is a quirky "museum" featuring caged fruit bats. Picturesque Praslin is a perfect place for painters – full of empty country roads, relaxed villages, red hills, distant islands and a deserted beach at the end of each

PRASLIN

▲ *Above: Zimbabwe Wilderness. So-named because 'it leads nowhere'.*

winding track. A number of artists live on Praslin, and many more make it their holiday retreat. The Café des Arts used to be run by artist Christine Harter, whose paintings actively encouraged all the visual arts in the islands. The Café is now a psychedelic technicolour dream bar linked to Le Duc de Praslin hotel overlooking the azure waters of the ocean.

Situated towards the eastern end of Côte d'Or is a large agricultural estate with palms, casuarina trees, mahoganies and browsing cattle. Years ago there was a tiny house here set on stone pillars that once belonged to Henri Dauban (*see* panel, page 109) who did so much experimenting with and development of farming techniques on this long, tree-filled flatland. A mangrove swamp survives in the corner, with crabs digging around in the cracked mud and small red, white and blue flowers growing on the sandy pathways. The birds fluttering cheekily at your feet are the *twoutwel coco* or barred ground dove, supposed to bring peace and good luck.

A long, isolated road goes past stands of passion fruit with their green, egg-shaped fruit and white tendril flowers, and reaches the elegant Archipel villas. From here a path leads along the wild and rocky coast around **Devil's Peak**, or Fond Diable ('fond', is an old French word meaning crown). This leads to delightful Anse La Blague which faces, across the reef, a coterie of lovely islands: Félicité, Petite Soeur, Grande Soeur, Île Cocos and the larger island of La Digue. A gear-challenging forested road leads over the hills from here to Baie Ste Anne.

CONSERVATIONISTS

For centuries, nature was considered boundless by the inhabitants of Seychelles. In 1769 Abbé Alexis Rochon was the first scientist to visit the islands. Twenty years later a true conservationist arrived, engineer and administrator Jean-Baptiste de Malavois. He made recommendations for the protection of Seychelles' timber, tortoises and turtles. Victorian artist Marianne North, Botanical Gardens director Paul Dupont, researcher and writer Dr John Bradley in the 1930s and Seychellois today such as Guy Lionnet, 'Kanti', Nirmal Shah, Justin Gerlach, Mia Dunford and Adrian and Judith Skerrett have much encouraged interest in Seychelles' flora and fauna.

VALLÉE DE MAI

Though Praslin is generously blessed with stunning beaches and a wonderfully laid-back atmosphere, the peculiar attraction of the island is to be found in a small area of thick forest high up in the green hills. Here the famous **coco de mer** tree has its last natural habitat, in a valley of 4000 slumbering giants known as the Vallée de Mai (Kreol-abbreviated to *Val di Me*). The valley, an area of only 18ha (45 acres) enclosed within Praslin National Park's larger 338ha (835 acres), is a World Heritage Site, one of only two in Seychelles.

The whole national park area was so remote and mountainous that it remained totally untouched until the 1930s – a saving grace for the indigenous trees. Trail leaflets lead you to some of these, including the *bwa rouz*, with leaves like corrugated cardboard, and *northea kapisen*, with its horizontal cracked-mud bark. The new Information Centre at the entrance to the reserve is where the well-laid-out circular path begins. The car park and Information Centre are approximately halfway along the mountain road between Grand'Anse and Baie Ste Anne.

Fifty-two of Seychelles' indigenous plants and trees can be seen in this extraordinary valley, including all six endemic palm species. It is the last habitat of the unique **black parrot** whose numbers at 600 are gradually and fortunately increasing; some on Curieuse and Denis islands. Unusual reptiles include the bright green **Praslin gecko**, the non-poisonous **wolf snake**, the **tiger chameleon**, and a fund of frivolous **frogs**.

The main attraction, however, is the coco de mer. As you walk into

▼ *Below: Deep inside the emerald-tinged Vallée de Mai forest.*

PARROT OF THE PALMS

The black parrot (*kato nwar*) is actually coffee-coloured. It whistles like a street kid, and mynah birds imitate it perfectly as it flies through the jungle of coco de mer palms in the Vallée de Mai. Although secretive and difficult to see, a flock of 30 are sometimes spotted in flight. It climbs with claw and beak and sometimes swings upside down from a male coco de mer catkin. A great fruit eater, it munches into anything from mangoes to figs or the bitter *bilenbi*. It has recently been declared a distinct unique species. The female can have two or three mates that feed her while she sits on her eggs. Clever lass.

the forest, the silence is overwhelming. Above and close around are the phalanxes of monstrous palms, soaring 30m (100ft) to a sombre canopy of knife-pleated fronds the width of a room, with clusters of nuts each as heavy as a suitcase. When a light breeze disturbs one of the looming trees, it fidgets and rasps its fronds against a neighbour, while a gust of wind will send the huge trees into a frenzy of clattering branches which sound like coconuts in a storm falling on a tin roof. Then, just as suddenly as it started, the great giants will rest again, reforming their eerie atmosphere of swirling, sunlight-pierced green light.

Ever since the coco de mer made its first, mysterious appearances around the fringes of the Indian Ocean, it has been the source of legend, wonder and erotic delight. The nut which grows on the shorter female tree looks like a gigantic green acorn, but husked, the black, hard-shelled double coconut strikes a remarkable resemblance to a woman's rounded bottom, while the 1m (3ft) long catkin, covered in yellow flowers, provides the male biological adjunct. Understandably believed to have aphrodisiacal and medicinal powers, the fabled nut commanded fortunes from princes and potentates around India and the Middle East. Sailors knew the coco de mer palm as the tree that emerged from the ocean and provided a nest for the mythical giant *rukh*, or roc, which had a 50m (150ft) wingspan and would carry off any unwary seamen who came too close. The Japanese considered the nut sacred, Indian princes fashioned them into jewelled drinking gourds, and one was even priced at 4000 golden florins.

Vallée de Mai

Pink Coco de mer
Shelter
Seat
Capucin Tree
Bridge
Bridge
Seat
Tallest Coco de mer
Bridge
Bois Rouge Grove
Japanese Bridge
Seat
Central Path
Lily Pond
Grove
Bois Rouge Grove
Seat
Car Park, Boutique, Tea Garden
N
Palm & Pandanus Grove
Entrance & Kiosk
Circular Path
Bois Mon Père
Viewing Point
Waterfall
BAIE STE ANNE
GRAND'ANSE

| 0 | 100 m |
| 0 | 100 yd |

Grove Plants
Footpaths

It was not long before the coco de mer aroused interest in a totally different way. General (at that time Colonel) 'Chinese' Gordon visited Praslin in 1881 and wrote a lengthy dissertation entitled *Eden and Its Two Sacramental Trees*. The breadfruit, he decided, was the Tree of Life, while the coco de mer was the Tree of Good and Evil. At a time when the theory of evolution was being hotly debated and Darwin excoriated, Gordon (like today's 'Intelligent Design' fundamentalists in America) believed in a literal interpretation of the Bible. He colourfully explained the Book of Genesis in terms of Praslin, the Vallée de Mai and the coco de mer palm. This explanation may not have found its way into mainstream theology, but nevertheless his theories were to become the pivotal drawcard of Seychelles tourism: the scented Garden of Eden, God's tropical paradise among the palms, islands of love a thousand miles from anywhere in the far Indian Ocean. And few can deny the effectiveness of the image.

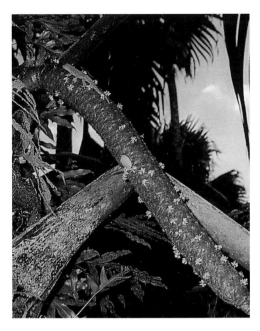

▲ *Above: The long, flower-speckled catkin on a male coco de mer palm.*

Praslin Island Walks

Praslin is small enough to ensure that cycling and walking are each an excellent way to get to know the island. There is not much traffic, it is relatively flat around much of the coastline, and there are plenty of quiet paths leading through old plantations and out to windswept viewpoints. Buses (with fares at SR5/US$50 cents) run regularly around the coastal road, so it is never difficult to get back to your hotel.

BLACK PEARLS

Smaller than the coco de mer but even more valuable is the Seychelles black pearl. These gorgeous droplets are cultivated at the aquaculture farm near Amitié airport. Known to the Chinese as the 'secret soul' of the oyster, pearls were first 'cultured' in 1896. Black pearls can be copper, gold or silvery blue and a trophy string can set you back US$200,000.

PRASLIN

▼ *Below: The round Praslin country road goes past sleepy Anse Marie-Louise, a delightful spot for handline fishing.*

Anse Possession: Leaving from **St Matthew's Church** in Grand'Anse, the narrow road passes the attractive Britannia Hotel and leads up into breadfruit tree patches scattered with rock-perched houses. At the saddle of the hill 140m up you can look out over the ocean to Mahé. From here the right-hand road heads towards Salazie and Côte d'Or, while the left-hand road follows the **Pasquiere River** down to Anse Possession, named by French sea lieutenant Lampériaire on behalf of Captain Dufresne in 1768, facing **Curieuse Island**.

Southern Tip: Another route is to go south out of Grand'Anse, carry on past the turning to Vallée de Mai, and walk along the coast road as waves crash against the sea wall at high tide, spray almost touching the palm fronds. Past the elegant Coco de Mer Hotel, where you might see a black parrot, there is a collection of delightful pocket-sized coves – **Cemetery**, **Boat**, **Consolation** and the larger **Marie-Louise** – each with high-rise cliffs. **Pointe Cocos** is the southernmost tip of Praslin Island; from here it is not too far over to **Baie Ste Anne**.

◀ *Left: Ocean rollers dashing against spectacular granite boulders frame the powder sands of Anse Lazio in Baie Chevalier.*

Baie Chevalier: One of the most pleasant walks (especially early in the morning) is to go north to Baie Chevalier. From Grand'Anse you walk past the new airport buildings at **Amitié** and the Black Pearl's giant clam breeding aquarium. **Cousin** and **Cousine** islands, the enchanting siblings of North Praslin, are 2km (1.2 miles) off the almost blinding snow-white beach. Near the end of the road there is a turn-off to the new Lémuria Resort which has unfortunately managed to cordon off three of the loveliest beaches on Praslin – Anse Kerlan, Petite Kerlan and Anse Georgette – to give exclusivity to its 18-hole golf course. (Do not be fooled by resort hotel regulations; everyone is allowed on any beach in Mahé, Praslin and La Digue – otherwise guests would presumably be confined to their resorts.) **Pointe Ste Marie** overlooks **Anse Kerlan**. A white handmade cross stands at St Marie's Point offshore of the resort in memory of a child who drowned here many years ago.

A mainly dirt road leads over the red earth hills of latanier palms and pandanus, past high ocean views to the cobalt blue and pristine curve of sand at Baie Chevalier's Anse Lazio, the quintessential pirate cove. Deep and reef-free, it is a popular yacht anchorage with an "Honesty Bar", and two restaurants, one revelling in the name of Bonbon Plume. From the restaurant a rough road proceeds to **Anse Boudin**,

PRASLIN

▶ *Right: Anse Lazio beach, voted one of the world's most beautiful. It now has an Honesty Bar on the sandy shore.*

SPICE ISLANDS

The first French settlers came to the islands to plant spices. Only cinnamon really survived, but the islands have been spicy ever since:
• Lemon grass, or *citronelle*. Long tufted green grass, lovely as a tea.
• Cinnamon, or *kanel*. Leaves look like spear tips, and are used with bark for cinnamon oil and in cooking. Used to be a major plantation industry, and still found everywhere.
• Patchouli. Its dried scented leaves were used instead of moth balls, and its oil is a fixative in perfume.
• Cloves. The prized spice of pomanders and chefs that countries went to war over.
• Plus nutmeg, vanilla, ginger, chillies, pepper and all the spice of life.

where the round-Praslin buses start up again. Or drive up to Grand Fond ('Zimbabwe') hill viewsite.

CURIEUSE

Curieuse Island, a kilometre off the northern coast of Praslin, lies within the Marine Park. The area is home to both fish and coral of every extraordinary variety and colour; snorkelling or diving in the clear, warm water is to feast on the silent wonder of the living reef.

The undersea garden here is to enter another truly wondrous world. Try it with a friend. Brain and stag corals, spiky black sea urchins, giant cowries, purple-lipped clams, and thousands of darting, flashing fish can all be seen. There are blushing brown octopus, razor-toothed barracuda, moray eels darting from their caverns, batfish, lovely blue and yellow surgeonfish, big horned and drowsy Picasso trigger-fish, and the needle-thin trumpet fish. Loveliest of all is the dappled brown hawksbill turtle, winging away in the blue. Many flipper up onto the beautiful white beach facing Praslin each year to lay their eggs. The park contains an abandoned turtle pond at Baie Laraie built 100 years ago but its muddy mangrove waters enclosed by a 500m (550yd) causeway across the mouth of the bay didn't meet the approval of the turtles.

The island, 3.5km (2 miles) long, named in 1768 by Lieutenant Lampériaire, Captain of the schooner *La Curieuse*, is a breeding centre for 250 giant tortoises, coco de mer palms and black parrots. It was originally called Île Rouge, its distinctive red soils laid bare by repeated fires. From 1833, Curieuse was a leprosy village – initially for sufferers and slaves released from Mauritius – until the discovery of the breakthrough drug Dapsone in the 1960s made it redundant. The ruins of the 1930s village can still be seen at Anse St José as well as the lovely *takamaka*-shaded double-storey Doctor's House built by Sir William MacGregor, the 26-year-old Scottish physician who came to Curieuse in 1873. His home, beautifully renovated by the daughters of Seychelles historian William McAteer, is now a museum and national monument. There are good walking trails round the island. The one that leads from the baby tortoise pens to Anse Badamier on the east coast, a well-forested area, will also enable you to branch off to 172m (564ft) Curieuse Peak. Trees on the trails are tagged and numbered.

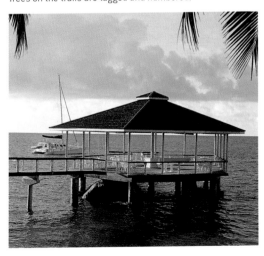

◀ *Left: At Anse Bois de Rose, Coco de Mer Hotel's jetty leads to a mid-sea pergola and bar.*

PRASLIN

COUSIN

Cousin Island, lying 2km (1 mile) from Praslin's Anse Kerlan beach, is a little island covered in indigenous *mapou* and *bwa torti* forest, and a designated Special Reserve. It was purchased by Birdlife International in 1968 and is now administered by **Nature Seychelles** to protect its endangered and rare birds, particularly the **Magpie Robin** and **Seychelles brush warbler** (*le petit merle des îles* in French). All birds are ranger-protected and colour ring-coded. Only 20 people at a time may visit.

Breeding **shearwaters**, large brown birds that bank low over the water between the waves, are protected on Cousin. Sometimes you can see 'rafts' of as many as a thousand sitting on the water fishing for squid or flying fish, returning to their nests in the evening moaning and groaning. White **fairy terns** with little blue-black beaks, **tropicbirds**, the little **yellow-capped fody** or *tok tok* (from the sound of its cry), and Seychelles blue pigeons are all common on Cousin. There are also 100,000 breeding **lesser noddies**, and the population of **warblers** has increased from only 26 left in the world to today's several hundred.

Hawksbill turtles come to lay their eggs on Cousin's beaches from August to April. They are the subject of the world's longest-running intensive monitoring programme of this species, with constant observation.

▶ *Right: A solitary waxy-leaved veloutier bush, characteristic of many a Seychelles beach, creeps towards the sea.*

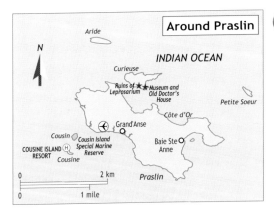

Around Praslin

Aride
INDIAN OCEAN
Curieuse
Ruins of ★ ★ Museum and
Leprosarium   Old Doctor's
House
Petite Soeur
Côte d'Or
Grand'Anse
Cousin
Cousin Island
Special Marine
COUSINE ISLAND ⓗ Reserve
RESORT   Cousine
Baie Ste
Anne
N
0   2 km
0   1 mile
Praslin

COUSINE PRIVATE NATURE RESERVE

'Hold tight,' the skipper calls as he turns the open boat towards the waves and beach. 'Just like the Quantum of James Bond.' And you roar through the pass and up onto the powdery white beach of tiny Cousine Island, truly a one-man-saved Garden of Eden.

Cousine's four villas, possibly the most luxurious of Seychelles' bevy of glamorous resorts, are not there to make money. Every cent spent on Cousine stays on Cousine to finance the granitic island – a dedicated nature reserve, a haven of conservation. There are 21 giant tortoises (three types altogether in Seychelles), each named (MacGregor, Gertrude, Junior), a host of breeding hawksbill sea turtles, the vulnerable Seychelles wolf snake (non-toxic), Wright's endemic skink, the green-day gecko, five species of butterflies, 20 types of ant, four different ghost crabs, and a continuous swirl of endemic birds including impish fairy terns, Seychelles warbler, Seychelles magpie robin, white eye, blue pigeon, nine species of tern sea birds, turtle doves, fody, sunbirds, shearwaters, noddies, frigate birds, crab plovers, curlews, sandpipers, and a list of 40 visitors and vagrants that pass by for a drink.

Nesting hawksbill turtles (*Eretmochelys Imbricata*) are are a feature of the island's pristine scimitar-shaped egg-laying beach and a priority for the island's resident and

PRASLIN

▲ *Above: The gravel road over to Praslin's Baie Chevalier looks out to Aride Island.*

devoted conservationists, often from different parts of the world. Millipedes are the star workers. Reaching a foot in length, they consume 17% of all available leaf litter on the island each day, forming a rich natural fertilizer and performing a vital function in soil production and nutrient cycling.

ARIDE

From banks of beautiful reefs and a tiara of white sand, Aride Island, 10km (6 miles) north of Praslin, rises in luxuriant guano-fed vegetation to a lovely plateau. It is a long green island of unbelievable beauty, which has been preserved from the planter's axe ever since it was first visited by man in 1756. The old Seychellois family Chenard owned it for 100 years and insisted it became a protected Seychelles sanctuary, which it soon did when purchased in 1973 by Christopher Cadbury of the chocolate family, and it is run today by Seychelles' Island Conservation Society.

Aride, even more so than Cousin, is Seychelles' great bird paradise. Only Aldabra boasts more varieties of breeding sea bird, and between May and October over a million birds lay their eggs on the island. It is home to more **lesser noddies** than anywhere else in the world, an unusual hilltop **sooty tern** colony (360,000 pairs) and a total of 10 species of breeding sea birds. Among the granitic islands, only Aride plays host to breeding **red-tailed tropicbirds**. There are also big populations of **white-tailed tropicbirds**, **fairy terns**, **shearwaters** and the huge, stealth-bomber **frigate birds**.

The English artist and botanist Marianne North, who came exploring the Seychelles in the 1880s, visited Aride to paint **Dr Wright's gardenia**. Known as *bwa sitron* in Kreol (it looks like a lemon), this shrub has a heavenly scent, trumpet-shaped white flowers flecked with magenta, and a hard round green fruit. Some 2000 still grow on Aride, but nowhere else on earth.

Aride is one of the most memorable islands in Seychelles. Visits (Sunday, Monday, Wednesday) to the island are controlled both by the warden and the weather, which can make landing difficult.

Aride's protected habitat has been a tremendous boon to Seychelles' endangered wildlife and plant species, particularly the four critically endangered endemic birds of Seychelles (*see* panel, page 94). Meanwhile, Aride's indigenous vegetation has taken on a new life with the cutting down of exotic fruit trees and coconut palms.

COCONUT SUPREME

There are two million coconut trees in Seychelles.
- The nut is eaten, squeezed into a cream, or even grilled as a cocktail snack.
- Perfume, margarine, soap and sunscreens contain coconut oil.
- The brittle shell, ground and turned into a charcoal paste, lubricates aircraft bearings.
- Mattresses, anchor ropes, and car seats all benefit from coconut husk coir.
- Mahé matrons in pre-Dyson days used to polish floors with a half husk underfoot and a flick of the hip.
- Seychelles shopping bags, heart-shaped fans and roof thatch all make use of the strong fronds.
- Tasty dainties include heart of palm salad, sweet germinating nut, and coco water.
- The sap of the tree, toddy or *kalou*, tastes like ginger beer. Leave it 12 hours and it will blow your head off.
- Coconut palm fronds serve as makeshift sails and beach picnic cloths.
- Coconut root is said to cure many ailments.
- *Poonac*, animal feed from the residue of oil extraction.
- Split husks are used to grill whole breadfruit, or as swimming floats for kids.
- *Tammy* is weaved into hats, sunshades and cooking filters.

◀ *Left: Amber-mottled jewellery from hawksbill carapace was known as tortoiseshell. Now banned.*

PRASLIN AT A GLANCE

BEST TIMES TO VISIT

Dec to **Feb** are rainy. It can pour down, but rainfall on Praslin is slightly lower than on Mahé. Temperatures remain fairly constant at 30ºC (86ºF) and humidity 80%. At night the temperature drops a few degrees. There's always a breeze of 6 to 7 knots increasing to 12 knots and more in **Jun** through **Sept**, the sailing season.

GETTING THERE

The cheapest way (US$20) is a fast (one hour) luxury Cat Cocos ferry from the inter-island ferry terminal, off Independence Avenue. (drinks and comedy TV aboard). Arrive 30 minutes beforehand. Same for flights.
Air Seychelles' daily domestic terminal flights every 15 minutes are enormously convenient, but the airline, strangely, charges much more for visitors than for locals.
Helicopter Seychelles (e-mail: reservations@helicopter.com) or Zil Air (website: www.zilair. com) shuttle will give you another view of paradise.

GETTING AROUND

There are comfortable *Tata* **buses** that circle the island every 45 minutes. Both sides of Praslin are relatively flat, and **bicycles** can be hired from Côte d'Or and Grand'Anse or borrowed from your guesthouse. There are **taxis** at both airport and jetty. For **car hire** try Grand Bleu, tel: 248 4 293960. But the best way to see Praslin is to **walk**.

WHERE TO STAY
Small Hotels
Family run and no bedside phone reading: "Anything. Anywhere. Anytime".
Chalets Côte Mer, Baie Ste Anne, tel: 248 4 294200, e-mail: ccmer@seychelles.net website: www.chaletcôtemer. com 12 rooms. Near ferry quay facing La Digue Island.
Amitie Chalets, Amitie Beach, tel: 248 4 233216, e-mail: martini@seychelles.net website: www.the-seychelles. com Four rooms.

Mid-range
Indian Ocean Lodge, Grand'Anse, tel: 248 4 233324, e-mail: iol@seychelles.net website: www.indianocean lodge.com 32 rooms; beach pool, pub and restaurant. Lots of character. Recommended.
Hotel Coco de Mer and **Black Parrot Suites**, Anse Bois de Rose, tel: 248 4 290555, e-mail: cocodem@seychelles. net website: www.cocodemer. com 52 rooms. There's always a warm welcome at this palm-fringed hotel. Excellent cuisine.
Village du Pêcheurs, Côte d'Or beach, tel: 248 4 290300, e-mail: village@seychelles.net website: www.thesunset hotelgroup.com Smart boutique hotel.
Le Duc de Praslin, Anse Volbert near Côte d'Or beach, tel: 248 4 294800, e-mail: leduc@ seychelles.net 24 rooms; another great hotel on Côte d'Or's strip.

Le Relax Beach Resort, Grand'Anse, tel: 248 4 233238, e-mail: beachresort@lerelax hotel.com website: www. lerelaxhotel.com 10 rooms. Island views.

Top Dollar
Acajou, Côte d'Or, tel: 248 4 232400, e-mail: acajou@ seychelles.net website: www. acajouhotel.com 30 tropical hillside villas overlooking glorious beach, gardens and views.
Hotel L'Archipel, Anse Gouvernement, tel: 248 4 284700, e-mail: archipel@ seychelles.net website: www. larchipel.com 30 rooms, tropical hillside garden setting. Recommended.
Paradise Sun, Côte d'Or, tel: 248 4 293293, e-mail: paradise@seychelles.net website: www.paradisesun. com 80 chalets, range of facilities. Idyllic beach location.
La Reserve, Anse Petite Cour, flanking Curieuse Marine Park, tel: 248 4 298000, e-mail: resa@lareserve.sc website: www.lareserve.sc 32 rooms (16 bungalows), candle-lit jetty and swim-up bar.
Raffles, Takamaka Bay, tel: 248 4 4296780, e-mail: praslin@raffles.com website: www.raffles.com/ praslin 86 hillside villas.

Budget
Beach Villa, beachfront Grand'Anse, tel: 248 4 233445, e-mail: martin@seychelles.net Nine rooms, ask for room 9.

Great sunsets. Recommended.
Islander's Guesthouse, Anse
Kerlan, tel: 248 4 233224,
e-mail: islander@seychelles.net
Self-catering. Eight rooms. Beach
was location for film *Castaway*.
Near Lémuria golf course.
Britannia, Grand'Anse village,
tel: 248 4 233215, e-mail:
britannia@seychelles.net
website: www.seychelles.
resa.com 12 rooms, excellent
Kreol food.
Îles des Palmes, Anse
Takamaka (N.E.), tel: 248 4
232941, e-mail: islands@
seychelles.net website:
www.beachbungalow.sc
18 bungalows, self-catering.
Cousine Island
Cousine has only four villas,
a sanctuary of silence for the
turtles and sea birds as well as
their guests. Just off Praslin,
tel: 248 4 321107, e-mail:
cousine@seychelles.net
website: www.cousineisland.
com Recommended.

WHERE TO EAT

Hotels and guesthouses have
restaurants. Also worth trying:
Café des Arts on Côte d'Or
beach, tel: 248 4 294800. Now
linked to Duc de Praslin. Beach
setting.
Bonbon Plume, Anse Lazio
north coast, tel: 248 4 232136.
On exquisite powdery beach.
Usually only serves lunches.
Black Parrot, Grosse Roche,
tel: 248 4 233034. Some say
this is the best restaurant in
Praslin. The first restaurant on
the island (50 years ago) was
also called the Black Parrot.

La Goulue Café, Côte d'Or, tel:
248 4 232223. Spicy fish curries.
Capricorn Restaurant, Anse
Kerlan, tel: 248 4 233224.
Closed Sun. Beach barbecues.
Meals at 'satisfying prices'.
Indian Ocean Lodge,
Grand'Anse, tel: 248 4 233324.
Good value Kreol cuisine.
Britannia Restaurant,
Grand'Anse, tel: 248 4 233215.
Small established Kreol
restaurant. Nice atmosphere.
**Airport Touchdown
Restaurant**, Amitié, tel: 248 4
233655. Serves snacks.

TOURS AND EXCURSIONS

Local tour operators offer many
options.
Cousine Island Bird Sanctuary.
Three-hour trips from Maison
Des Palmes Hotel, Grand'Anse.
Tues–Fri, 09:30–12:00 and
14:00–16:00. Not open
holidays. No restaurant, no
overnight, no swimming, no
smoking, lots of mozzies.
Check with your hotel for week-
day sightseeing from a boat,
eg *Papillon*.
Curieuse Marine Park. Day
boat trips with lunch can be
organized through any hotel or
tour operator. With a snorkelling
stop at St Pierre Islet.
Diving (and learning to dive).
PADI courses, night dives, and

wonderful coral and sea life in
Curieuse Marine Park; 8 dive
centres on Praslin, try Octopus,
Côte d'Or, tel: 248 4 232350.
Water Sports. Catamaran sailing, hobie cats, paddle skis,
windsurfers, etc. Particularly
Côte d'Or. Some hotels have
their own equipment.
Vallée de Mai National Park.
Tour operators undertake tours
around the home of the coco
de mer. Or, take a taxi or bus,
get a map with your entrance
fee and do it yourself. **Golf** at
Lemuria's 18-hole golf course.
Bus. Catch one, take a picnic
to the cove of your choice.
Tours from Mahé. Tour operators' day trips to Praslin include
hotel pickups, air or sea cruise
transfers, and transport to
Vallée de Mai, Curieuse Marine
Park, Cousin, or Aride Island.
Other tours combine Praslin
and La Digue.

USEFUL CONTACTS

Air Seychelles: tel: 248 4 284666.
Tourist Office: tel: 248 4
233346 (airport). **Health**:
Clinic at Grand'Anse, small
hospital at Baie Ste Anne, tel:
248 4 232333. **Tour Operators**:
Mason's Travel, tel: 248 4
288750, or Creole Travel
Services, tel: 248 4 233223.
Emergency: 999.

PRASLIN	J	F	M	A	M	J	J	A	S	O	N	D
AVERAGE TEMP. °F	81	82	82	82	82	81	79	79	79	81	81	79
AVERAGE TEMP. °C	27	27.5	28	28	28	27	26	26	26.5	27	27	26.5
SEA TEMP. °F	82	80	82	80	78	77	73	73	73	79	77	80
SEA TEMP. °C	28	27	28	27	26	25	23	23	23	26	25	27
RAINFALL in	12	7	6	5	5	4	2	4	5	6	7	12
RAINFALL mm	295	172	160	124	135	116	53	99	130	141	179	311
Days of Rainfall	9	5	6	6	6	3	3	4	4	5	5	10

5
La Digue

"Don't let's go to the dog's tonight" sums up chunky and different La Digue. The 3000 La Diguois consider their island a separate republic. Here wedding parties travel in decorated oxcarts, everyone else by bicycle, including schoolchildren returning home on their parent's cross bars. There is no airport (although there is a helipad), they rely on ferries and schooners to connect with the rest of the world, men go shirtless and shoeless, and even the Kreol language can be different.

La Digue, the fourth largest of the granitic islands, yet only 5km (3 miles) by 3km (2 miles) at its widest, lies a short ferry hop from Praslin's Baie Ste Anne. It is still the most traditional of the islands, although that and the addictive rural atmosphere does make it increasingly attractive to visitors. There are dozens of tiny self-catering bungalows with exotic roadside names, exquisitely sited hotels and beachfront guesthouses. La Digue is well within range for day trips from Praslin. Once on the island there is nowhere more than an hour's walk away, and a bicycle (with supermarket shopping basket) will cost you less than US$8 to hire. There is a colourful boutique off every dirt road.

La Digue is dominated by the 333m (1093ft) **Eagle's Nest** mountain and a broad, and at times marshy, agricultural plain on the western side where most of the population lives. The island has spectacular black granite boulder formations, particularly along the beaches, curving and grooved as if by the hand of a giant sculptor. At times they can appear almost

◄ *Opposite: La Digue at sunset, with Praslin in the distance.*

LA DIGUE

DON'T MISS

★★★ La Veuve Paradise Flycatcher Reserve and Takamaka Trail through the 10,000 trees forest.
★★★ A ride in an oxcart. There are two private contractors.
★★ A bicycle ride along the paved coastal road. Stop for tea at Patatran Hotel.
★★ Early morning walk through the mountain forest to Grande'Anse.
★★ Snorkelling, fishing, sight seeing trip on a small boat.
★ Keven Jeanne's shoreside Fish Pond research centre.
★ Château St Cloud, and its tortoise pen. Stay for supper.
★ Barbara Jenson Art Studio.

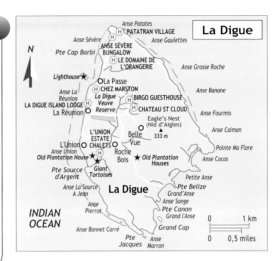

SCHOONERS

Sailing has always been a part of Seychelles, from the Arabs in their dhows, who were the first to record the islands, to the age of pirates and naval rivalry. The ferries that sailed between Mahé, Praslin and La Digue in days of yore were often romantic schooners. Sometimes with a half-truck strapped to the fore deck. When the breeze piped it was exhilarating, sails taut and the crew in their yellow oilskins grinning as they hauled in bonito with cotton handlines. The womenfolk were guided below as the crew presumed they were more prone to be seasick.

pink in colour. The beaches, inevitably, are wild, lonely, and beautiful. With a cat's cradle of tangled palms and *takamakas* leaning madcap over every gorgeous beach, colourful old tin houses, white waves dashing against granite boulders, and haunting sunsets, it is also the prime destination for fashion magazines, photographers and movie men. *Robinson Crusoe* was one of several films shot on the island. La Digue is also the major remaining habitat of the gorgeous Seychelles Black Paradise Flycatcher, *Terpsiphone corvina*. The male boasts long black tail streamers.

La Digue is one of ten granitic islands grouped around Praslin. **Félicité**, to the northeast of La Digue, has a lodge located on its largest beach, but no other habitation. It is the island where the Sultan Abdullah of Perak (Malaysia) was exiled in 1876. The waters surrounding Felicité are known for their winged manta rays, *diable de mer*. They are the harmless gentle giants of the deep and not at all devilish.

AROUND LA DIGUE

La Passe

La Passe, the main settlement on La Digue, takes its name from the one gap in the island's encircling reef which the schooners from Praslin use to get to the coral pier. In among the palms and *takamakas* arching over the road, which flanks Anse La Réunion beach south of the pier, are several colourful landmarks including Tarosa Café, the library, Chez Marston restaurant, and STC Supermarket, which apparently has so many more goodies than Mahé shops, that it has bequeathed La Digue with a new laconic nickname: Dubai. A little further on you reach La Digue Island Lodge, one of two sizeable hotels on the island, then the handsome 1854 Assomption church and the turnoff to La Digue Paradise Flycatcher Reserve. The wide road ends at L'Union Estate which has the largest vanilla plantation left in Seychelles. The atmosphere is so unhurried it is difficult to believe much has changed since the first inhabitants, political exiles from the island of Réunion (near Mauritius), settled here and whose old graves can be seen in the cemetery at Cap Barbi.

Behind La Passe, visitors can find one of the real La Digue experiences in **Château St Cloud**, the old St Ange family house overlooking Eagle's Nest mountain. It is a 90-minute walk from the Château up the Belle Vue road to the summit of the island, **Nid d'Aigles** (which means Eagle's Nest, although there have never been any eagles in Seychelles).

Grand'Anse

A road crosses the island from the estate at L'Union to La Digue's version of Grand'Anse, and it is a popular uphill walk past quaint little stalls selling mountain fruit juices. The flat lands are full of the island's traditional air, with a lone cow being led out to graze, maybe an old plantation house at the end of a long avenue of palms, all rusting grey tin and decaying arrogance, and such non-Dubai enterprises as Villa Mon Rève guesthouse,

▼ *Below: Patatran Village Hotel overlooks lovely Félicité Island.*

LA DIGUE

▲ *Above: A lovely smile from a little island girl. Arab, Indian, African, European and Malagasy blend perfectly in the Seychelles people.*

Lucy's Trading Store and good value Gala Takeaway. On La Digue you are more likely to see the old plantation equipment and skills (such as rapid-fire husking of coconuts on a stake in the ground) than anywhere else. Despite the increase in tourism, traditional industries such as patchouli, vanilla, copra, saffron, boat building and fishing are still very much a part of La Digue's way of life.

A huge old casuarina tree surrounded by grass and green *veloutier* bush stands sentinel on Grand'Anse, framed at either end by massive pinkish-black, grooved granite boulders. The beach faces the blustering southeast trades, and looks out towards Frégate Island, a blue silhouette in the ocean.

Apart from the ghost crabs scurrying in the foaming surf there may only be a few pairs of wheeling fairy terns, a long-beaked turnstone, or a whimbrel, which migrates 10,000km (6200 miles) from Siberia. Though the sea, without the barrier of the coral reef, seems dramatic and inviting, take note of the multilingual warning sign about the currents.

The East Coast

The track east through the palms goes over a small hill to another equally deserted and beautiful beach, **Petite Anse**, and then on along a series of thundering surf beaches framed by lush forested mountains. La Digue's famous pink granite boulders are strewn around the edges of all these east coast beaches, giving colour both to the sand and the sparkling water lapping around their feet. One of the beaches, **Anse Caiman** (Crocodile Beach), is where the fearsome reptiles ambushed the first 1777 French families to settle on the island.

At **Anse Fourmis** the island's circular road begins again, weaving in and out of forest, coves, rocky outcrops and deserted beaches. It rounds the northern tip, where the views over the beaches **Anse Gaulettes**, **Anse Patates** (and its alpine Patatran Village Hotel) and **Anse Sévère** are a continuous delight, before leading back to La Passe.

Pointe Jacques

South from L'Union beach, a path leads to **Anse Source d'Argent**, epicentre of La Digue's snorkelling and beach rock formations, then to **Anse Pierrot** and **Anse Bonnet Carré**, up to Pointe Jacques, the southerly tip of the island, where you will either have to scramble along the shore or over the headland. North from here is a beach, **Grand l'Anse**, with a small island just off it, where the path becomes clearer, and soon joins the main road over the island between Grand'Anse itself and L'Union.

▼ Below: Dawn reveals sculpted burnt orange rock formations at Grand'Anse beach.

LA DIGUE VEUVE RESERVE

The plateau on La Digue between the mountain and the sea is dominated by Indian almond (*badamier*) trees, *takamakas* and wetland. The marshes are the habitat of the **Seychelles black paradise flycatcher**, one of the most endangered birds in the world. And consequently steadfastly protected on La Digue. The male is blue-black from crown to the tip of its long streamer tail. The shorter-tailed female is more colourful. The best place to see them is the tiny La Digue Veuve Reserve (*veuve*, or commonly just *vev*, which means 'widow' in Kreol, is the local name for the flycatchers).

The 21ha (51-acre) reserve is not far from Château St Cloud. Set up in a bid to save an area

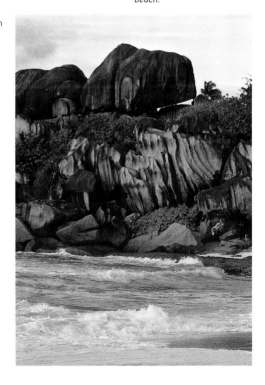

LA DIGUE

Seventeen bird species are endemic to Seychelles, but as with many island inhabitants, they are all endangered.
• Seychelles blue pigeon. At a distance it looks like a fish eagle; has a 'ko-ko-kok' cry.
• Seychelles kestrel, or *katiti*, a tiny bird of prey that hides in the eaves of houses.
• Seychelles scops owl, or *syer*. This bare-legged resident of the high mountains is rare and seldom seen.
• Seychelles black paradise flycatcher. Some have been translocated to other islands, but mainly found on La Digue. The white and chestnut female is different from the blue-black of her mate.

▶ *Opposite: Elegant Château St Cloud Hotel.*
▼ *Below: With luck you may still see an old schooner off La Digue.*

of natural habitat for the birds, the reserve has an information centre, a nature trail, and a permanent ranger. In the lily pools you might see the pale brown and orange **lily trotter**, or Chinese bittern, stalking across the swamp in search of some tiny bream or frogs. The ranger will also point out the best place to spot the rare **yellow-bellied** and **star-bellied terrapins**, known as *torti soupap* to the Seychellois, another species sadly endangered by the gradual draining of the marshes. These web-footed reptiles live in freshwater pools and marshes, and eat both plants and snails.

On the road leading down from the reserve to **L'Union** on the coast, there are more lily ponds and mangroves where you might spot some wild orchids. L'Union Estate's theme park (and thatched self-catering chalets), beneath a canopy of soaring, twisted palms features a magnificent plantation house, old coconut oil mill, copra dryer, and giant tortoise pen. It is well worth the small entrance fee. The boatyard specializes in wooden fishing boats. *La Bousir* sells snacks and souvenirs.

LA DIGUE ISLANDS

There are four small islands all within a radius of 7km (4 miles) of La Digue: Marianne, Félicité, Grande Soeur and Petite Soeur, plus the La Fouche and Coco islets. The **Sisters**, to the east of La Digue, are deserted. The larger has two attractive beaches either side of its hourglass middle. There is good fishing all around them, especially for barracuda and wahoo.

Félicité Island

This island, halfway between the two sisters and La Digue, was, for five years in the late 19th century, the home of the exiled Sultan of Perak. These days isolation carries a healthy price tag, as it is probably the only place in the Seychelles outside the Amirantes where you can hire an island all to yourself. Accommodation (16 persons) until recently was in two plantation houses. Boasting 'six senses *zil pasyon*', so if you have a passion for fishing, go for the waters around the nearby islets, Île Cocos.

The island was a plantation run by the Cauvin family for many years and then the favourite holiday spot for presidents and princes. Félicité mountain rises steep above the little hook of beach and chalets, with a path to its 231m (758ft) summit, lush with gnarled old *takamaka* trees and coconuts, and some heart-stopping granite cliffs down to the sea.

Marianne Island

Named after one of the ships which came to Seychelles 200 years ago, Marianne is uninhabited. It is thickly covered in coconuts but conservationists are hoping that the native forest will gradually return. There are some fine rock formations in the south, which can be seen from a boat, that are perhaps even better than La Digue's panoramic sculptures. The darting Seychelles sunbird *kolibri* is there in profusion.

CHÂTEAU ST CLOUD

This 200-year-old, two-storey grey and white stone château – with creaking takamaka floors polished with *mangliye* (extract of mangrove), shuttered windows and only four luxury rooms (plus hillside chalets), overlooking banks of flowers, breadfruit trees and a giant tortoise pen – would not be out of place in Provence or Blois, the regions of France the St Ange family left to come to Seychelles 200 years ago. In the elegant open dining room Myriam's chefs produce a feast that only island women could devise. Myriam, of Reunion descent and the 16th generation in Seychelles (her father was a Government Minister, and her brother, Alain, is today Minister of Tourism and Culture), still oversees every detail of the Château.

LA DIGUE AT A GLANCE

BEST TIMES TO VISIT

During the **December** to **February** rainy season, the low-lying plateau of La Digue where most of the hotels are sited can be very wet, with some parts flooding. The best times to visit are **April** to **September** when it is less humid and the southeast trades are blowing. Because of its dense forests it always seems more tropical on La Digue. The temperatures, in the main, are the same as the other granitic islands, an average of 27ºC (81ºF) and 80% humidity.

GETTING THERE

There is no airport on La Digue, but there is a **helipad** at the coast with regular shuttle services. The normal route is to fly by plane to Praslin and take the comfortable Cat Rose **catamaran** which leaves Praslin's Baie Ste Anne anchorage several times a day, or a **schooner**, to splice the mainbrace and experience a whiff of the salty sea and surging waves – *Ah, me hearties, Drake be in his hammock and a thousan' mile away*. Check days and departure times for any sea crossings from Mahé direct to La Digue. Praslin to La Digue is only 5km, so if you are into Xtreme sports, you can, with a local expert, windsurf across.

GETTING AROUND

There are now few of the old creaking **ox carts**, the historic method of transport for guests and their luggage, but you can order one for special occasions. They are pulled by Brahman bulls. **Bicycles** can be hired practically anywhere, especially at hotels. There is only one circular road around the island. Plus several others in the village. All are paved and carefully swept by residents each early morning. You can hire a bicycle for SR100 per day.

WHERE TO STAY

La Digue has many colourful self-catering establishments. All family run. They include:

Small Hotels
Pension Michel Garden Guest House, Anse Réunion, tel: 248 4 234003, e-mail: pm@seychelles.net website: www.pensionmichel.sc Eight rooms in a gorgeous flowering garden.

Top Dollar
Château St Cloud, inland of Anse La Réunion, tel: 248 4 234346, e-mail: stcloud@ seychelles.net website: www.seychelles.net/stcloud 22 rooms, four in the enchanting old two-storey plantation residence. Run like an elegant country inn at the time of the French Revolution, it also has its own resident giant tortoises.

L'Union Estate Chalets, tel: 248 4 292525, e-mail: reservation@ladigue.sc This is the most expensive accommodation on La Digue by far. It consists of eight units on an old plantation with a secluded beach. Basically self-catering.
La Digue Island Lodge, Anse Réunion beach, tel: 248 4 292525, e-mail: reservation@ladigue.sc 69 thatched A-frames.
Patatran Village, Anse Patates, tel: 248 4 234333, e-mail: patatran@seychelles. net website: www.patatran seychelles.com Bird's-eye bungalows overlooking ocean and islands. Swimming pool. Recommended.

Budget
Chez Marston, tel: 248 4 234023, e-mail: mars@ seychelles.sc With its five new rooms near the jetty, Marston maintains the quixotic 200-year-old St Ange tradition of hospitality.
Anse Sévère Bungalow, North La Digue, tel: 248 4 247354, e-mail: clemco@ seychelles.net One only self-catering beach bungalow, a 15-minute bicycle ride from La Passe.

Most small hotels and guest-houses are near La Passe.

Islands
Félicité Island
Félicité is a gem. Accommo-modation for 16 persons,

so one party can have it all to themselves, tel: 248 4 292525 or 4 234366. Félicité has decided to flaunt itself as '*zil pasyon*'. Wow!

Note: there are no accommodation facilities on Marianne and Les Soeurs. However, day visitors can go to any of these islands. Check with tour operators or your hotel.

WHERE TO EAT

Zerof, Anse Réunion, tel: 248 4 234067. Kreol food. Ring to book.

Le Tournesol, La Passe, tel: 248 4 234155. Small eatery, great fish curries.

Chez Marston, Anse Réunion, tel: 248 4 234023. Good food, and good conversation.

Patatran Village, tel: 248 4 294300. Deserved reputation for live music and for tasty Kreol food.

Château St Cloud, tel: 248 4 234346. Elegant French-Kreol cuisine.

TOURS AND EXCURSIONS

Local tour operators on La Digue will assist you with any excursion, hotel booking, bicycle hire or holiday activity. Their offices are at La Passe jetty as you get off the schooner. As is the Tourist Office, tel: 248 4 234393, open during office hours.

Helicopter Trips. Shuttle services from Mahé, La Digue, scenic flights and charters all available. Also to Félicité and Cousine, tel: 248 4 385863.

Diving. There are at least eight dive centres on Praslin and one on La Digue: Azzura Pro Diving at La Digue Island Lodge, Anse Réunion, tel: 248 4 234232. Good La Digue dive sites include Anse Marron Bank, Anse Sévère (photography). Surrounding islands' dive sites include: Aride Bank, Wolfgang's Wall (Curieuse) and South Marianne.

Sailing. Hobie cats and windsurfers. Check at the Tourist Office or your hotel.

Fishing. Barracuda, wahoo, tuna, and bonito are plentiful, particularly between Félicité and Les Soeurs, while fishing in a small boat off the reefs is exhilarating. All hotels and guest houses have a favourite fisherman and all can arrange fishing trips.

Rock Climbing. Has not really taken off in Seychelles. If you have you own gear, try Pointe Jacques or Source d'Argent.

Snorkelling. Equipment for snorkelling can usually be borrowed at your hotel.

Horse riding. Short beach rides only at L'Union Estate as the horses are unshod. C/o La Digue Island Lodge, tel: 248 4 292525.

Oxcart trips. Inexpensive and available anywhere along the main roads; a leisurely way to see the countryside and meet the villagers.

The **La Digue Festival** takes place on 15 August each year, Assumption Day. It is a grand day with bunting, processions, music, feasting and festivities. It is very popular, attracting folk from Mahé and Praslin, as well as practically all the residents of La Digue.

USEFUL CONTACTS

Air Seychelles, tel: 248 4 284612 (Praslin).

Telephone Enquiries, tel: 100.

Emergency (Police and Fire), tel: 999.

Emergency Hospital, tel: 151.

Tourist Office, tel: 248 4 234393.

Mason's Travel, tel: 248 4 288857.

Creole Travel Services, tel: 248 4 297000, e-mail: info@travelservices.com

Inter-Island Ferry, Catrose, tel: 248 4 232329, e-mail: iif@seychelles.net

La Digue Island Lodge: tel: 248 4 292525.

Marine Charter (Mahé), tel: 248 4 322126.

LA DIGUE	J	F	M	A	M	J	J	A	S	O	N	D
AVERAGE TEMP. °F	81	82	82	82	82	81	79	79	79	81	81	79
AVERAGE TEMP. °C	27	27.5	28	28	28	27	26	26	26.5	27	27	26.5
SEA TEMP. °F	82	80	82	80	78	77	73	73	73	79	77	80
SEA TEMP. °C	28	27	28	27	26	25	23	23	23	26	25	27
RAINFALL in	12	6	7	6	5	3	3	5	6	8	6	12
RAINFALL mm	315	149	178	146	129	84	87	124	124	203	154	313
Days of Rainfall	9	5	6	6	5	3	3	3	3	4	5	9

6
A Pattern of Islands

From granite mountains to coral specks, huge atolls to little more than a ring of sand and a solitary palm, the 115 islands of Seychelles stretch like a string of pearls across 1000km (620 miles) of the Indian Ocean. Away from the main island group around Mahé and Praslin, the Seychelles archipelago quickly becomes remote and unknown, yet these Outer Islands are as rich as their more populous siblings, and just as valuable a part of the vivid tapestry of Seychelles.

The vast majority are uninhabited, and visitors common on just a few. To get to some of them is both difficult and adventurous, but for that the rewards seem all the greater. Their names, **Amirantes**, **Alphonse**, **Farquhar** and, possibly the most fascinating of all, **Aldabra**, are ones to conjure up images of wildness and wonder, endless sky, sea and floating islands. They are places where nature is still strongly in command, where unique plants and unusual animals cling to a thin thread of existence, not always threatened by man, but often simply by the wheels of nature itself.

BIRD ISLAND

Bird and Denis are the two most northerly of the Seychelles islands. Chagos lies 1930km (1200 miles) to the east, and the Maldives 2250km (1400 miles) to the north. Bird Island is a nugget of coral, palms, turquoise tropical sea and a million breeding sea birds.

As you get off the Otter aircraft after a half-hour flight from Mahé, the manager is there to greet you and soon over

Amirantes Group · Mahé

Alphonse Group

Aldabra Group · INDIAN OCEAN

Farquhar Group

CLIMATE

The **rainfall** is higher in the granitic islands of Silhouette, Frégate and around Mahé than in the hotter and drier coral islands like Denis, the Amirantes chain and the great atolls of the south: Farquhar, Cosmoledo and Aldabra. Farquhar can experience **cyclones** in the northwesterly monsoon from December to February. Very few of the coral islands have the forests of the granitic group but all have shady palms and casuarinas, and as low islands in a wide sea they have refreshing **breezes** whatever the season.

◀ *Opposite: Romantic beaches, romantic islands.*

A PATTERN OF ISLANDS

DON'T MISS

★★★ Staying at a remote and luxurious island lodge. The islands become all yours.
★★★ A few days with the birds on Denis or Bird Islands.
★★★ A sail to the Amirantes – each evening a new island.
★★ The thrill of fishing for sailfish and marlin.
★★ A walk on coral mushrooms on Aldabra.
★★ Scuba diving – corals and fish in crystal clear water.
★★ Silhouette's Dauban mountain: lush mist forests and magical untouched flora.
★ Frégate Island: your best chance for pirate treasure.

▶ *Opposite: Cool breezes and palm trees surround the bungalows of Bird Island.*

a welcoming fruit drink to explain that the essence of Bird is in what it does not have: no air conditioning, no TV, no telephones in the rooms and no need to lock anything away. And the long bar is a piece of East Borneo camphor wood washed ashore one stormy night.

Bird Island was originally called Île aux Vaches, after the dugongs, or sea cows, that early French explorers found here. Although there are no dugongs left, there certainly are birds. The island is an endless whirl of them: **fairy terns**, with blue-black beaks and eyes gleaming out of a cloak of white, perch in cuddling couples in the eaves of your bungalow; grey-brown **noddy terns** dominate the seashore, and between May and October each year 850,000 pairs of chattering, crying and wheeling black-and-white **sooty terns** arrive to breed and sit on their speckled eggs.

Each guest receives a check list which includes the common **crab plover**, **sanderling**, **great frigate** and **wedge-tailed shearwater**. In addition, dedicated ornithologists can hope to see the **black cuckoo**, **broad-billed sandpiper**, **corncrake** and an endless range of migrants and vagrants. Whenever you walk on the island there is the cry of sea birds.

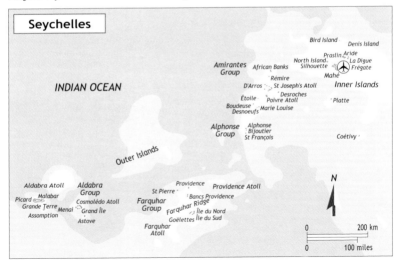

They nest up trees, on the beach, and even the Lodge is shaped like a giant frigate bird.

Around Bird Island

At the northern sandbank on the island the open flat beach reveals nothing but sooty terns. They dive and hover a metre above you, their masked faces curious and inquisitive. Their nest is a simple open 'scrape' of sand; if you are gentle they will allow you to get quite close. Before the island was declared a wildlife sanctuary in 1986, this placid attitude was exploited by egg collectors. There are six major sooty tern colonies in Seychelles: on Bird, Aride, Desnoeufs, Cosmoledo, Farquhar and Denis.

Bird Island only covers 69ha (170 acres), and at most it takes two hours to walk around its encircling white-on-white beach with smooth grey driftwood sticking up out of the sand. Sky blue waters surround the island which is bounded by jagged reef at **Passe Hirondelle** on the eastern side. Turtles come up on the beaches to lay their eggs, the hawksbill quite often during the day. Everything is carefully recorded.

One friend you'll definitely make is **Esmeralda**, the island's pet tortoise. Weighing in at 298kg (657lb), Esmeralda (she is actually a he) is recorded in the *Guinness Book of Records* as the largest tortoise in the world and at over 170 years, the second oldest.

OMELETTES, TERNS AND CROCS

The owner-managers of Bird Island are true conservationists. For them, turtles were not for harpooning, shells were for the seashore and sooty tern eggs were for the birds, not gourmet omelettes. They have seen the island's bird population grow from 20,000 to a million. Breeding hides for tropicbirds were created, Seychelles sunbirds introduced and the beaches have become a haven for egg-laying turtles. They have won conservationist and responsible tourism awards, have had to deliver at least one baby, and assured an Italian couple that green geckos were not baby crocodiles. A salinity-reduction system for coral atoll wells was invented on Bird.

A PATTERN OF ISLANDS

▲ *Above: Blue skies, a million birds and silent seas – Bird Island.*

DENIS ISLAND

'We had come to our island home at last,' Denis islanders will quote you. Governor Sweet-Escott, doing his round of the islands by boat in 1903, came to Denis, the guano-rich, and hence verdant, coral island 50km (31 miles) east of Bird. There he found that the lighthouse was 'in capital order and the quarters of the lightkeeper very much improved'. The lighthouse, refurbished in 1910, is still there but the accommodations have changed out of all recognition. The 25 sumptuous air-conditioned villas (inside and outside showers), each with its own private beach and almost invisible from each other, are run by owners Mickey and Kathleen Mason. Their son Alan now runs Mason's Travel while Mickey develops the island's agricultural base. It is the only Seychelles island other than Mahé to produce its own fresh milk, and using drip irrigation supplies all Denis' vegetable and fruit needs, as well as those of Praslin's Indian Ocean Lodge. The list includes pawpaws (20 large ones on each tree), jamalaks, bananas, breadfruit, mangoes, golden apples, passionfruit, limes, oranges and, of course, palmiste and coconuts, extracting oil from the latter and bottled for sale. The Masons have introduced cattle, pigs, ducks, quails, breeding tortoises, rabbits and 2000 chickens. One-seventh of the island's 350 acres is being left as original woodland while another area has been cleared to encourage migratory sooty terns to settle and breed. The Masons have replanted thousands of indigenous trees in the lush forests once decimated by guano mining.

Denis was named after sea captain Denis de Trobriand, who anchored off its ring of blue water and snowy beach in

DEEP-SEA FISHING

Game, or fighting fish, such as black marlin, blue marlin, tuna, wahoo, bonito and barracuda, are all found in Seychelles' waters, along with the prince of them all, the sailfish, which features on Seychelles' coat of arms. The best months for sailfish are March to June, October and November. A number of boats are available to charter for fishing, with skippers who know the waters well. Speak to Marine Charter, or head for Denis or Bird's close-in fishing grounds.

his vessel *L'Etoile* on 11 August 1773, en route to India. Sited on the edge of the Seychelles Bank, which disappears into a 2000m (6500ft) abyss, the island has become very popular with deep-sea fishermen as the fishing for marlin and sailfish is always good. Denis has several unusual touches: an abandoned prison, a cemetery, a chapel, and some unusual coastal coral formations known as the Caves.

SILHOUETTE

From popular Beau Vallon Bay on Mahé's west coast, gorgeous Silhouette rears as a mist-shrouded pyramid in a silvery sea. Seychelles' high-forested answer to Bali Hai in the South Pacific, and a ghostly wonder at every dazzling sunset. Only 19km (12 miles) from Mahé, it is the third-largest island in the archipelago, and the only one with mist forests as high as those on Mahé. The highest point is the 740m (2428ft) Mount Dauban. Silhouette gives its name to Air Seychelles' in-flight magazine, but the name of the island in fact came from a French finance comptroller, Etienne de Silhouette, rather than from its moody, darkened profile.

COWRIES

Of the 165 known species of cowrie, a mollusc, 50 can be found in Seychelles.
• Cowries are the homes of living creatures that feed on algae. The fleshy mantle of the animal creates the hard, glossy shell.
• The name originates from the Hindu word *kauri*; the shells have often been used as a form of currency.
• Two of the most common cowries in Seychelles are the Tiger and the Arabian cowrie.

▼ *Below: The aquamarine seas and talcum white sands of Denis Island.*

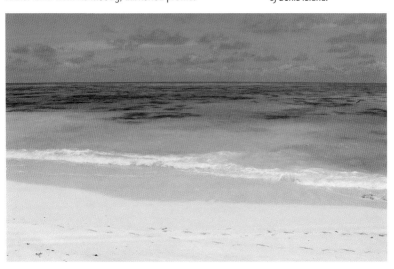

A PATTERN OF ISLANDS

Silhouette was owned for many years by the Dauban family (the double-storey Plantation House is now a restaurant), and has therefore been relatively untouched by both the planter's axe and the developer's foundation stone. Before helicopters and the 52-seater Labriz motor launch that docks to chilled cocktail fruits and champagne, getting to Silhouette was a hazardous affair. Judging the swell and the jagged coral of La Passe was an exercise fraught with danger.

A thousand years ago the island was known to Arab seamen from the East Indies (or *lascars*, as they are called in Seychelles). Graves and ruins at Anse Lascars are believed to be of Arab origin but it will probably take sophisticated archaeological examination to confirm this. Ships of the English East India Company sighted Silhouette in 1609, while 200 years later Le Corsair Hodoul spent some time here. It is claimed (as it is for practically every island in Seychelles) that he buried treasure on one of its beautiful beaches.

Around Silhouette
Silhouette is roughly round in shape, 5km (3miles) long by 4km (2.5 miles) wide, and is completely surrounded by

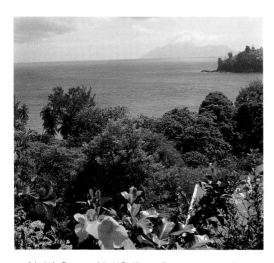

◀ *Left: Often capped in mist, pyramid-peaked Silhouette Island dominates every view from northwest Mahé.*

reef. Labriz Resort with 110 villas, a fitness centre and spa challenges Silhouette's Forgotten Eden idyll somewhat. Until recently, no money was used on Silhouette and there were only 200 inhabitants, a clinic, a school, and at Anse Grand Barbe, a lovely church.

Mont Dauban mountain is a tropical mist forest crammed with botanical treasure, including the rare pitcher plant with its secret juices which dissolve insects. Tiny orchids and rare hardwoods such as *bwa rouz* and *bois de natte* grow there, while the rare incense tree *bwa sandal* is found only on Silhouette. Other Silhouette specials include the *trilepisium madagascariense*, or false fig tree, discovered in 1883 on Mont Dauban, probably by the indefatigable Marianne North. The Nature Protection Trust of Seychelles (concentrating on tortoises) and the old plantation house are at La Passe. Nearby is a lovely lagoon surrounded by palms and mangroves. High in the lush rocky mountains, on the trail from **La Passe** to **Grand Barbe**, you can see fruit bats hanging from the trees or gliding like prehistoric pterodactyls, the sun catching the leathery sheen of their wings. There are a number of trails on the island, around the rocky coast or up through the thick, mostly untouched high forests.

DAUBAN, QUIXOTE OF SILHOUETTE

Buried in an impressive Grecian-columned mausoleum on Silhouette are generations of Daubans who have owned and run the island since 1864. Auguste Dauban, who fought at Waterloo, was the first to settle here. For much of the 20th century his bachelor descendant Henri Dauban, a tall, gaunt planter, intellectual, and environmentalist, ran Silhouette. A graduate of the London School of Economics, he joined the British Olympic javelin team in 1924, despite the fact that he was a Frenchman. He was an expert pirogue builder and excellent chef. The old family plantation house, built of indigenous hardwoods, still stands at La Passe on Silhouette.

A PATTERN OF ISLANDS

▶ *Right: Squabble and scrape, gaggle and haggle – sooty terns by the thousand. Go too close and you'll get pecked.*
▶▶ *Opposite: Nearly all hotels in Seychelles bedeck visitors' beds with delicate frangipani and hibiscus flowers, like this one on Frégate Island.*

NORTH ISLAND

The first Westerners other than the Portuguese to set foot on Seychelles did so on North Island in 1609 when Englishmen from the *Ascension* landed. Led by Commander Alexander Sharpeigh of the East India Company, the longboats brought back the giant tortoises to eat that John Jourdain, whose diary records the islands for the first time, claimed looked 'soe uglie before they were boyled'.

Tiny North Island is today a castaway retreat for the platinum wristband set. You could purchase Seychelles' annual production of cinnamon bark for a 16-night stay at the smartest of the eleven villas, with personal butler, plunge pool, massage bed, hot and cold running chefs, and organic (naturally) veggies. Don't feel bad: the lodge guarantees all is eco-friendly and in harmony with nature. **Grand Paloss** mountain (214m; 702ft) dominates North Island while paths lead to the plant nursery (with 70+ species) and four beaches including **Cimitière** (Cemetery), recalling the days when a child would often die before the men could row a huge hardwood pirogue the 25km (15 miles) of deep swell ocean to Mahé.

FRÉGATE

This lovely island of only 3km² (1.2 sq miles) is the most remote of the dozen granitic and hence mountainous islands that surround Mahé, a distance of 56km (34 miles) to the west. It used to have the only game on Seychelles – Asiatic deer imported from Mauritius. Its main exports since it was first explored in 1744 by French surveyor Lazare Picault have always been rum, copra, cashew nuts, vegetables and above all, the hint of pirate treasure.

Unlike Silhouette, North, or even La Digue, it has an airstrip and there is an elegant one-couple-one-villa-with-a-view lodge on airy cliffs overlooking blue seas. The old plantation house is now one of two restaurants offering fine Kreol cuisine. The ambience is Balinese, the luxury sybaritic and the *objets d'art* could only have been collected by someone fond of collectibles. It has jacuzzis, rock spa, aromatherapy and its own marina.

As to buried treasure, me hearties, Frégate comes tantalizingly close to the real thing. The island's first visitors were 18th-century buccaneers seeking refuge from marauding colleagues and the yardarm nooses of French and British men o' war. A sunken well lined with lead, ruins, cannonballs and gold have all apparently been found, and coral tombs have been reported. In 1812 a cross-

CORAL REEF FISH

There are 1000 species of reef fish in Seychelles:
• Parrot fish: bright blending colours. Named after their parrot beaks.
• Razor fish: thin, pencil-like creatures that swim in a vertical handstand position.
• Blue angelfish: a flat, square fish with iridescent blue edging to its wings.
• Moorish idol: gorgeous zebra markings and white top streamer.
• Batfish, or *pouldo* in Kreol. As large as a tennis racquet, they will swim alongside you.

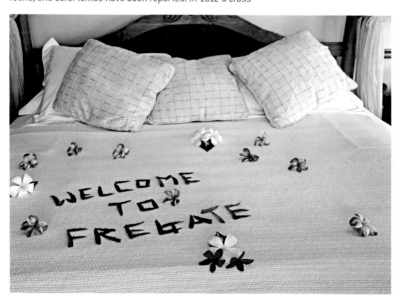

A PATTERN OF ISLANDS

belt and shoulder strap were unearthed, while in 1838 one visitor recorded that 'Spanish piastres and other coins called cruzados have been found on the shore ... with calm weather one can distinguish, half a mile from land, the debris of a large ship which lies at the bottom of the sea'. Careful research may yet reveal that all these finds are linked to the Arab seamen who crossed the Indian Ocean in their graceful dhows a thousand years ago, a treasure trove for archaeologists at least, if not bounty hunters.

In the hinterland are lovely forests, their luxuriant trees the favourite crawling territory of Frégate's unique **giant tenebrionid beetle**, which looks like a steel-plated version of the African dung beetle.

Birders come to Frégate, with its seven lonely beaches (particularly Victorin, often voted the world's best, an accolade Seychelles beaches seem to swap exclusively among themselves) and promontories of weather-grooved rocks, to spot the once nearly extinct **Seychelles Magpie Robin**. In 1970 they were critically endangered and almost extinct. Now there are nearly 300, many on Frégate, some on e.g. Denis where it is called the 'bird of pride'. They are tame ground-feeders with a blue sheen and white feather patches seen as they fly. Seychellois call them '*pti Santez*', the little singer.

▼ *Below: A manta ray glides into the deep blue.*

◀ *Left: Hibiscus, the quintessential island flower, is often used to decorate visitors' beds and also to make perfume.*

AMIRANTES

'And after some months here we fight, perhaps a bit feebly, against a desire to forget about the world at large.' So wrote New Yorker Wendy Veevers-Carter in 1966 about life on **Rémire Island** in the fabulous Amirantes, a chain of tiny coral atolls covered with palms in the middle of the Indian Ocean. Tragedy struck Veevers-Carter when her husband died on a trip to East Africa; being so remote she only learnt of his death weeks later. Their bungalow, now in ruins, stands facing the pass in the reef on this lovely island, now the occasional retreat of Albert René, the former president.

Rémire is only one in a cavalcade of 25 islands stretching south across 100km (62 miles) of ocean halfway between Mahé and Aldabra. From **Boudeuse** ('the sulky one') to **Marie Louise**, **St Joseph** with its cluster of islets thick with coconut palms, and **D'Arros**, the horizon seems to promise a new island every time you raise anchor. To visit these emerald jewels in a magic sea is an experience that will haunt you forever.

The Amirantes were known to Arab seamen and were named in 1502 in honour of Vasco da Gama (*see* panel, page 113). It takes 24 hours to sail the 250km (155 miles) from Mahé to Rémire, the faint tuft tops of palms being the first hint of land on the horizon, a warning not always heeded, as there have been many wrecks in the Amirantes.

Vasco da Gama

Less than a decade after Columbus had reached the West Indies, Portuguese navigator Vasco da Gama set out to find a seaborne route to the East Indies in a bid to break the Arab stronghold on the spice trade. His first voyage in 1497/8 took him round the Cape of Good Hope and up the East African coast – where a Chinese fleet had been 60 years earlier – before crossing to reach the coast of India at Calicut. He was made an admiral (hence 'Amirantes', named after him) just before his second voyage, which took him to Goa, an Indian enclave to become the centre of Portuguese power in the East for the next 500 years.

A PATTERN OF ISLANDS

▲ *Above: A deserted sandy road winds through an old coconut plantation, Desroches.*

One of the earliest recorded was that of *HMS Fire* in 1801, after which one Lieutenant Campbell, the commander, successfully sailed to Mahé in a canoe to get help.

Although airstrips have been built on several of the islands, only four are inhabited, and **Desroches** alone has been developed. A luxury lodge (with golf practice range) and a satellite ground station enable this island to lay claim to being 'the doorway to the Amirantes'. Its copra plantation is still working, and timber and charcoal are sent to Mahé. There is a small village of around 50 people while the lodge has 20 chalets and offers some exciting water sports, especially diving and fly bonefishing.

Many islands are not inhabited at all, bar a few adventurous 'Ilois', although at one stage or another most have been exploited for coconuts, green turtle, shark, timber, green snail (mother-of-pearl shells) and, above all, guano. The removal of this dung deposited by tens of millions of birds over thousands of years (particularly during the last ice age when millions of sea birds fled south) has badly affected some islands, leaving them covered with a coral pavement which one has to break through to reach the water table.

The uninhabited 35ha (86-acre) **Desnoeufs**, with a sooty tern colony three times that of Bird Island, was formerly the source of vast quantities of eggs, though now the island is enjoying a degree of protection as a breeding reserve.

Poivre

Poivre, the largest of the Amirantes islands, is named after Pierre Poivre, the man who encouraged the planting of spices in Seychelles. He is to be distinguished from Pierre

PIERRE POIVRE

His name literally translates as Peter Pepper, but perhaps he is more (mythically) remembered as Peter Piper, the man who picked a peck of pickled pepper. A peck was a barrel which had a volume of about 9 litres (2 gallons). He was the first Intendant on the Île-de-France, the name of Mauritius during French rule. He believed that on both Mauritius and Seychelles he could grow spices to compete with the lucrative trade that was being conducted between the East Indies and Europe.

Poiret, the man who claimed to be the true heir of Marie Antoinette and Louis XVI. Poiret farmed on the island between 1804 and 1822. A long lagoon, rich in bird song and lush vegetation, cuts into the atoll. To pole the length of this lagoon in the early morning, with fairy terns wheeling above the trees, waders strutting, an occasional turtle rising and perhaps even a giant guitarfish wriggling away beneath your boat, can be magically evocative. At low tide you can walk across the sand from La Pointe to Poivre Island itself, where handsome *bwa blan* trees shade the manager's sparse *La kaz* (cage) house. Accommodation on Poivre is very basic.

ALPHONSE GROUP

The smaller Alphonse group of atolls, three in all, lies 90km (56 miles) further south and 400km (250 miles) from Mahé. **Alphonse** itself is a shovel-shaped island of extraordinary beauty surrounded by perfect coral reef gardens. Small paths circle the island; at either tip, Dot and Tamatave, there are shipwrecks. **Bijoutier**, which means Jeweller, and **St François** complete this cluster. There is now an airstrip and lodge on Alphonse.

▼ *Below: A giant clam nestles menacingly in coral. These clams can be nearly a metre wide and their shells are often used as blessing fonts outside churches in Seychelles. They are farmed on Praslin Island.*

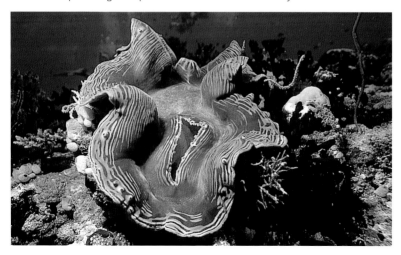

A PATTERN OF ISLANDS

▼ *Below: The World Heritage Site plaque at the settlement on Aldabra.*

FAR OUT ISLES

Île Platte (Flat Island) and Coétivy are in the opposite direction to the Amirantes from Mahé, and roughly as far away. **Platte** is renowned for its fishing and broad sandy beaches at either end of its 1.5km (1-mile) length. It seems to emerge as if from nowhere out of a vast expanse of ocean, and many a mariner has come to grief on its reef.

Coétivy covers an area of 931ha (3.5 sq miles), a thin island 10km (6 miles) long and one of the most productive islands both from sea and land in Seychelles. It was from Coétivy that the restaurants of Mahé used to get their tiger prawns, the delicious *krevet*. Sadly they are no longer available. Pork, beef, copra, fish, fruit, lamb and an abundance of vegetables are produced on the agriculturally rich soil of Coétivy, something that visitors have noted for years. In 1859 Bishop Vincent Ryan recorded that there were spacious pigsties on the island with 'immense animals in them', while the coconut mill employed 45 donkeys.

The island was first visited by a French sea captain named Coétivy in 1771. The old building ashore has thick walls and doors carved out of heavy *takamaka* wood. Many new buildings have been added to meet the hi-tech agricultural output of this island. Tourists as such do not visit this hard-working, functional island, although the island has both an airstrip and boat landing stage.

ALDABRA

Aldabra, the world's largest raised atoll and largest sea lagoon, is made up of a rugged ring of coral tufted with thick scrub. It sits atop a volcanic base and is surrounded by turbulent reef that slides, as if down a mountain slope, into the depths of the sea. Some 34km (21 miles) long and 14.5km (9 miles) across, the land area of the 14 islands encircling the ring of the lagoon is only slightly less than that of Mahé, although its lagoon alone could almost swallow the mountainous main island. It lies 1200km (750 miles) from the granitic islands, and about half that from mainland Africa, a distant, unique sanctuary for ancient animals, flora and marine life.

The shallow **lagoon** is dotted with umbrellas of coral that emerge like mushrooms at low tide to provide landing pads for booby birds. The lagoon, lined with mangroves, empties in a tidal rush every 12 hours through three main passes. At these times it is impossible to make headway in a boat against the turbulence. Yet, in the evening or early morning, and particularly when one of Aldabra's sudden squalls builds up across the lagoon, the shallow water can be a panorama of pastel colours quickly softening the mirror of heat from sea and sky.

Aldabra, rising an unusually height (for a coral island) 8m (26ft) above the navigator's horizon, was named by Arab seamen over 1000 years ago. Aldabra

GETTING TO ALDABRA

The nearest airstrip (there are no regular services) is on Assomption, a three-hour boat ride away. There are only a handful of scientists manning the research station, although at one time there used to be turtle hunters and even Chinese sea cucumber gatherers. There are no visitor facilities, but you can buy Aldabra T-shirts at the Settlement. Permission to visit the atoll can be obtained from the Seychelles Islands Foundation. P.O. Box 853, Victoria, Mahé, Seychelles, e-mail: sif@seychelles.net

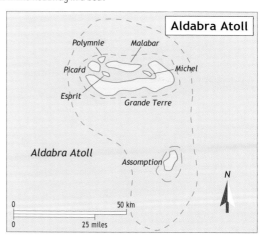

Aldabra Atoll

Polymnie Malabar
Picard Michel
Esprit Grande Terre

Aldabra Atoll

Assomption

N

0 — 50 km
0 — 25 miles

A PATTERN OF ISLANDS

could be a version of 'al-khadra', Arabic for the cloud reflecting green off the lagoon, but it could also refer to the heavenly constellation, Aldebaran. In 1964, Aldabra was nearly flattened to build a joint British-US airbase. Conservationists worldwide, alerted by Seychellois leaders, raised the alarm and Aldabra's rare wonderland was saved. Today it is a World Heritage Site and wonder of nature 'given to humanity by the people of Seychelles'.

Flora

Aldabra is no verdant honeymoon isle of silvery sands and whispering palms. Covered in ragged **pemphis scrub**, with the occasional line of **casuarinas** and twisted **palms**, the weather-ravaged surface of the steel grey-coloured coral is like a moonscape of ferociously pitted molten limestone. At the edge of the lagoon the undercut cliffs hang over the water, and when the southeast trades blow, whipping up the water, spray blows up through the holes like angry geysers. Despite the semi-arid desolate feel, however, Aldabra has been described as a living laboratory with 273 species of flowering shrubs and ferns, 19 of which grow only on this fabulous atoll.

Apart from the Aldabra **screw pines** (or *bwa damand*) and huge stands of mangroves that line the lagoon, a number of species advertise their rarity with the prefix Aldabra in their name. Two, as if cocking a snoot at their harsh environment with sweet fragrances and delicate flowers, are **Aldabra jasmine** and the **Aldabra lily**. The two areas on Aldabra where the landscape is a little more gentle are along the fringes fertilized by sea-bird guano where gnarled **mapou trees** grow, and among the sand dunes in the south.

▼ Below: Old graves of turtle-hunters and Chinese sea cucumber gatherers on Aldabra.

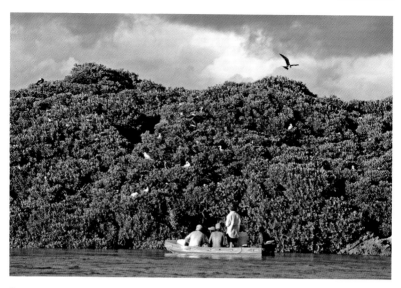

Fauna

Birds, of course, are born to fly. The few flightless species around the world tend to be household names, with the solitaire of Rodrigues and the 'dead as a dodo' of Mauritius perhaps the best known of all. In the Indian Ocean, however, all are dead and gone, except for Aldabra's **white-throated rail**, the little olive green and rather tame bird that pecks about the bush. Rare, though rather unspectacular to look at, the rail is joined by the unique **Aldabra drongo**, with its forked tail, and the skulking **Aldabra warbler**.

In addition there are thousands of other **terns**, **tropicbirds** and **boobies** rising from the mangroves. The boobies are known as *fou* (daft) in Kreol, possibly because they are easily frightened into disgorging their catch by bullying **frigate birds** who breed in tens of thousands on Aldabra. **Flamingos** can be seen, as well as the striking **Aldabra sacred ibis**, while the **Aldabra souimanga sunbirds** are far more colourful than their granitic island cousins. The **Aldabra fruit bat**, with its distinctive white face, cruises in the evening among the trees.

▲ *Above: Boobies are persecuted by frigate birds. But in the mangrove thickets fringing Aldabra's lagoon, they uniquely co-nest.*

THE ALDABRA GOATS

Among the incredible and unusual wildlife on Aldabra, the last thing you would expect to find is a plain old goat. The Aldabra goats are a throwback (so old salts say) to the days when the British navy would drop off a couple of the hardy animals, and perhaps plant a few coconut trees on remote islands so that shipwreck victims had some hope of survival when they drifted onto the inevitable desert island.

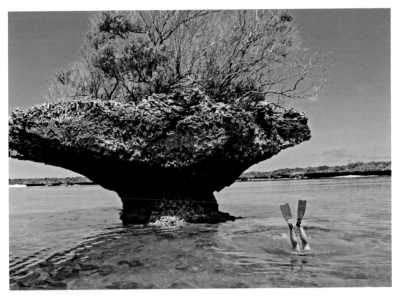

Possibly the strangest of all creatures on this living museum is the large **robber** or **coconut crab**. This reddish-pink, sometimes green monster, a land-breathing crab which can grow up to 60cm (2ft) long, likes to hide away under rocks and scuttle up coconut trees at night to rip open green nuts with its huge pincers.

DINOSAURS

Although they can swim quite well, it is unlikely that the Aldabran tortoise came to the atoll from the Galapagos, halfway around the world and the only other natural habitat of giant tortoises. On land, they can manage 30m (100ft) an hour, but this unstressed attitude pays off, as they can also go for weeks without food, and have been reported to live for 150years. The tortoise goes back to dinosaur days, a species even older than the sea-faring crocodiles that used to terrify early Seychellois settlers.

The Aldabra Group

Cosmoledo atoll, Astove and Assomption Island are part of the Aldabra group. **Cosmoledo** is a 19km (12-mile) atoll broken up into 12 islands, whose reefs are littered with wrecks. Sailing close to the ring of islands can be hazardous as its landfalls (with names such as Wizard, Mosquito and Pagoda) are widely separated but linked by silent deadly reef. The harvesting of turtle, guano and green snail (mother-of-pearl) denuded Cosmoledo of much of its flora and fauna, although the atoll is still very attractive. A million pairs of sooty terns among other birds are the only inhabitants of Cosmoledo.

Astove is a ring atoll with only one break into its beach-lined lagoon. Centuries ago a group of slaves lived here in freedom for 40 years after their ship was wrecked on the atoll's reef. Today's few inhabitants make reed brooms for Mahé. Astove offers fabulous fishing to the favoured few.

Assumption, to the west of Cosmoledo and 27km (17 miles) south of Aldabra, is the staging post for Aldabra, with a landing strip for small aircraft, and accommodation available. Once another great source of guano, these days its sand is highly valued by the construction industry on the Inner Islands.

FARQUHAR GROUP

Farquhar, 710km (440 miles) south of Mahé can be lashed with terrible tropical cyclones that sneak across the Indian Ocean from the northwest during the months of January and February. Winds of up to 120 knots ('just beginning to turn me on' as Seychelles yachtsman Brownie will tell you at Victoria's yacht club) howl across the two largest islands and their great circlet of reef, whipping the palms and cutting a swathe of destruction like a scythe across the islands. Underwater the terrible convulsions of the ocean heave and crash the corals as if in an avalanche. No wonder

CORAL ATOLLS

One of Charles Darwin's aims during his circumnavigation on the *Beagle* was to determine the formation of coral atolls. His view (which is still widely recognized) is that atolls are the final stage of a continuing upgrowth of coral around a sinking volcanic island. Coral is also always growing outwards from the centre of an atoll, favouring the ocean-facing side where plankton is richer than in the water of the lagoon.

◄ *Opposite: Aldabra's mid-lagoon mushroom-shaped coral formations attract the attention of a snorkeller.*
▼ *Below: A yacht delivers visitors to remote Assomption Island.*

A PATTERN OF ISLANDS

▼ *Below: Noddy ponders his nest for the night.*

that Farquhar (discovered in 1504 by João de Nova, the Portuguese navigator) and its neighbour Providence have the deadliest shipwreck record in Seychelles, some 12 in all. In the 20th century alone, Providence has been responsible for the loss of the *Jorgen Bank*, the *Endeavour, SS Syria* and at least one schooner, the *Maggie Low*.

However, make it past the treacherous reefs and strong currents of the narrow pass into the Farquhar lagoon, and it is one of the safest and loveliest anchorages in the islands. Farquhar is lush with palms and casuarinas growing down to white beaches. There is a settlement there, a phone, a seldom used airstrip, and a simple island house which can be rented to visitors through the Islands Development Company (idc@seychelles.sc).

The group takes its name from Sir Robert Farquhar, a governor of Mauritius, and in fact these islands were only transferred from Mauritius to Seychelles in 1921. Only Providence and Farquhar are inhabited.

BEST TIMES TO VISIT

The granitic islands in particular have heavy rains in Dec and Jan. The coral islands receive less rain but it can be erratic with sudden, heavy showers any time of the year. It is less humid on the coral islands and there's usually a sea breeze. Bird-watching is best from Apr to Oct, fishing from Oct to Apr, and diving from Mar to May and Sept to Nov. Farquhar can suffer cyclones.

GETTING THERE

Aircraft or helicopter transfers to and from the islands are organised by the resorts, including the private islands of Alphonse, Anonyme, Bird, Cousin, Desroches, Frégate, Félicité, North, Denis Island and Ste Anne's.

Amirantes: There are 10 islands in the group. Flights to Desroches, or 24 hours by yacht. Contact the following yacht charter companies: Blue Safari, e-mail: blue safari@seychelles.sc Elegant Yachting, e-mail: elegant@ email.sc Island Charters, e-mail: info@islandcharters.sc Seafever Charters, e-mail: info@ seafevercharter.sc Cruising the Amirantes by yacht is magnificent. Astove, Bijoutier, Coétivy, Cosmoledo, Farquhar, Platte and Poivre are managed by the Islands Development Co. (IDC). Incoming boats must apply for permission to visit: Port and Marine Services Division, e-mail: marineservices@ seychellesports.sc Coétivy is

a productive agricultural island. Permission is needed to go there.

Aldabra: *Indian Ocean Explorer* (info@ioexpl.com) can be chartered from Nov to Apr. There is an airstrip on Assomption. Seychelles Islands Foundation, sif@seychelles.net

GETTING AROUND

The normal means of transport is to **walk**. Longer trips to the far side of the larger islands would normally be done by small boats with an outboard engine.

WHERE TO STAY

Lodges or resorts are often the only accommodation on an island; generally they are small, luxurious and exclusive.

Alphonse Island Lodge (Coralline), tel: 248 4 322682, e-mail: alphonse@seychelles. sc 30 thatched A-frames in Amirantes.

Bird Island Lodge (Coralline), tel: 248 4 323322, e-mail: reservations@birdisland seychelles.com website: www.birdislandseychelles.com 24 chalets.

Desroches Island Resort (Coralline), tel: 248 4 229003, e-mail: reservations@des roches-island.com website: www.naiaderesorts.com Superb diving.

Frégate Island Private (Granitic), tel: 248 4 670100, e-mail: info@fregate.com website: www.fregate.com 16 rooms, seven beaches. Luxury living for the bird and beetle boffins.

North Island (Granitic), tel: 248

4 293100, e-mail: info@north-island.com website: www. north-island.com Villas, spa and connoisseur's cellar.

Denis Private Island (Coralline), tel: 248 4 288963, e-mail: reservations@denisisland.com website: www.denisisland.com 25 exquisite beach chalets separated by lush foliage. Azure coral seaviews.

Hilton Seychelles Labriz Island, tel: 248 4 293949, e-mail: sezlb.info@hilton.com website: www.hilton seychelleslabriz.com/ Champagne welcome.

WHERE TO EAT

All those islands with lodges have excellent kitchens. Other than boutiques in these lodges, there are no shops.

ACTIVITIES AND EXCURSIONS

Day trips by helicopter or boat, and occasionally by aircraft, are possible to some of the islands. Fishing, sailing, diving, snorkelling and nature walks are usually offered at all the islands with lodges.

USEFUL CONTACTS

Indian Ocean Explorer Cruises, tel: 248 4 225844, e-mail: info@ioexpl.com

Islands Development Co. (IDC), tel: 248 4 224640, e-mail: idc@seychelles.sc

Seychelles Islands Foundation, tel: 248 4 321735, e-mail: sif@seychelles.net

Nature Seychelles, tel: 248 4 601100, e-mail: nature@seychelles.net

Travel Tips

Tourist Information

Seychelles maintains Tourist Offices in the following countries around the world, among others:

France (Paris),
tel: 33 1 4453 9320, e-mail: info@tourismeseychelles.com
Germany (Frankfurt), tel: 49 69 2972 0789, e-mail: info@seychelles-service-center.de
Italy (Rome),
tel: 39 0 6509 0135, e-mail: info@seychelles-stb.it
South Africa (Cape Town),
tel: 27 21 426 0104, e-mail: seychelles@stoza.com
Spain (Madrid),
tel: 39 41 702 0804, e-mail: info@turismoseychelles.com
UAE (Dubai),
tel: 971 4286 5586, e-mail: seychelles@stome.ae
Seychelles Tourism Board, The Seychelles Islands, Another World, tel: 248 4 671300, e-mail: info@seychelles.travel
website: www.seychelles.travel/

Air Seychelles

Air Seychelles has sales offices or GSA's in:
France (Paris),
tel: 33 1 4289 8683;
Germany (Munich),
tel: 49 89 5525 3338;
India, tel: 91 11 2335 0295, e-mail: kg@tracrep.com
Italy (Rome), tel: 00 39 06 509 8413;
UK (Crawley), tel: 44 1293 596 656/5;

South Africa (Johannesburg), tel: 27 11 781 2111;
South Korea, tel: 82 2 6399 6927, e-mail: consul@seychellestour.co.kr
Qatar (Doha),
tel: 974 441 1414;
and in 37 other countries.

Entry Requirements

A valid passport is required but Seychelles does not require visitors to obtain visas. Ideally you should have a return ticket and a hotel booking. Seychelles Immigration is the epitome of visitor-friendly. They know only too well where their *pain* is buttered.

Health Requirements

Airport ebola check, otherwise nil. Seychelles has no malaria, cholera, typhoid, bilharzia, yellow fever or ebola. Occasionally Dengue (symptoms like malaria).

Customs

Duty-free allowance: 400 cigarettes, 2 litres of spirits and 2 litres of wine per person. Spearguns, firearms, agri-cultural products, animals and drugs (other than person-al medicinal) are absolutely forbidden.

Travel to Seychelles

Mahé is the only port of entry. Air Seychelles flies

from London, Paris, Rome, Johannesburg, Beijing and in partnership with Etihad Airlines from dozens of other hubs. All yachts must contact the Harbour Master, e-mail: hm@seychelles.sc

Travel in Seychelles

Car hire is best. The **bus** service is good but seldom extends beyond 19:00 on Mahé and 17:30 on Praslin. **Taxis** are plentiful but quite expensive. There are only three traffic lights in Seychelles (one at Praslin airport) and seriously hairy drop-offs on all mountain and rural roads on Mahé. **Bicycles** can be hired, particularly on Praslin and La Digue. Air Seychelles has regular inter-island **flights** as does Helicopter Seychelles. Cat Cocos **catamaran** (150-seater) operates to Praslin and smaller craft from Praslin to La Digue.

Clothes: What to Pack

Bring your swimming costume, a broad-brimmed hat, umbrella, sun barrier, dark glasses, binoculars, 2-pin adaptor and snorkelling gear. Long trousers could be needed for the evening.

Money Matters

There is no exchange control in Seychelles. The Seychelles

Rupee (around SCR14/15 to US$1) was floated on the open market (to the detriment of locals) in 2010 and the rupee is used everywhere. The Seychelles Rupee, which is divided into 100 cents, comes in denominations of SCR500, SCR100, SCR50, SCR25 and SCR10. There are **banks** with ATMs on Mahé, Praslin and La Digue; they are open from 08:30–14:00 and on Saturdays 09:00–11:00. Airport banks are open for some flights only. There is no black market in forex. As they say in Kreol, *ki pou fer?* what to do?

Tipping. Restaurants and hotel bills usually include a VAT charge, but a tip for good service is always appreciated.

ACCOMMODATION

The **largest hotels** are cocoons of high-density amenities, restaurants and luxury, usually on the best package holiday beaches, ideal if you want to stay put. There are smaller, more exclusive, hotels on Mahé, Praslin and La Digue. There are also a large number of 'Affordable Seychelles' **smaller hotels**, **guesthouses** and **self-catering** establishments which are the best way to pick up the flavour of the islands. Many book into these for three nights and then look around. There are luxury 'one-island-one-resort' **lodges** on Anonyme, Cousine, Frégate, Félicité, North, Silhouette and Praslin's Round Island but

the best are such outer coral islands as Bird, Denis and Desroches. The government initially set a limit of 5000 hotel beds in Seychelles, a number which has been considerably exceeded. Prices range from US$130 (B&B for two persons) to US$4000 per night. Truly. There are **no camping facilities** anywhere on the islands and if you're on a budget, stick to the smaller or self-catering establishments and travel by bus. Again, it is advisable to have proof of booked accommodation. *No sleeping on the beach, guys*. And then you will be given a month's visa, renewable at the Department of Immigration in town. Nearly all hotels and guesthouses serve excellent meals, and there is a wide selection of **restaurants** mainly concentrating on Kreol and French cuisine. Seafood dishes predominate. Count on US$40 per person. Cheapest take-away is about US$4.

TRADING HOURS

Shops and businesses are closed on Saturday afternoons and Sundays, although some rural shops open at odd hours over the weekend and late in the evenings. Normal business hours are 09:00 to 16:00 with a one-hour break, 12:00 to 13:00, when some will shut.

MEASUREMENTS

Seychelles uses the metric system throughout.

GOOD READING

Accouche, Samuel: *Once Upon a Time, a Soungoula*. (1976) Folk tales.
Amin, Mohammed et al: *Aldabra*. (1995) Superb coffee-table book.
British Navy: *South Indian Ocean Pilot*. (1971) Essential for yachties.
Brown, James: *Adrift*. (1981) True story novel.
Bulpin, TV: *Islands in a Forgotten Sea*. (1969) Travel.
Burridge, Glynn: *Voices: Seychelles short stories*. (2000)
Grimshaw, Brendon: *A Grain of Sand*. (1996) A Robinson Crusoe life.
McAteer, William: Outstanding 3 volume *Seychelles History*. (2008). *Echoes of Eden*. (2014) This coffee-table book is a must.
North, Marianne: *A Vision of Eden*. (1993) Victorian botanist and artist.
Penny, Malcolm: *The Birds of Seychelles*. (1974)
Skerrett, Adrian and Judith: *Beautiful Plants of Seychelles*. (1991) Also bird books.
Tingay, Paul: *Night of the Rukh*. (1975) Adventure novel.
Tirant, AR: *Echoes from the Oasis*. (2010) Historical love story.
Travis, William: *Beyond the Reefs*. (1959) True diving adventures.
Veevers-Carter, Wendy: *Island Home*. (1970) A family alone on Rémire.

COMMUNICATIONS

Cable and Wireless have provided Seychelles with a superb **telephone**, **fax** and **e-mail** system, albeit the telephone directory is not fully comprehensive. There

are payphones everywhere (usually using cards which can be purchased at C & W, post offices, and other general outlets). GSM has a **mobile network** plus roaming. Mobile starter packs are available from C & W and Airtel (airport, tel: 248 4 600600). Paradise FM supplies the latest pop music while SBC broadcasts **TV and radio** in Kreol, English and French. *The Nation* is the official daily, and there are oodles of advertisement-packed booklets and flyers. Seychelles stamps are colourful and often treasured by collectors. There is a philatelic bureau at the main post office near the clock tower in Victoria. The international code for phoning Seychelles is 248.
Emergencies (ambulance), tel: 151;
Directory Enquiries Cable & Wireless, tel: 181;
Emergencies, tel: 999.

TIME DIFFERENCE
Seychelles time is GMT + 4.

ELECTRICITY
240 AC; 3-pin (square) plugs.

MEDICAL SERVICES
There is an excellent **hospital** at Mount Fleuri, near the Botanical Gardens, with X-ray, pathology, and all facilities, tel: 248 4 388000. Private **dental services** are available, tel: 248 4 224852 or 248 4 224354. There are **small hospitals or clinics** at many of the little villages on Mahé, Praslin and La Digue.
Private medical doctors include: Dr KS Chetty, tel: 248 4 321911 and Dr H Jivan, tel: 248 4 324008.
Pharmacies:
Foch Heng, tel: 248 4 322751 (after-hours tel: 248 4 241233); Behram's, tel: 248 4 225559; George Lilams, tel: 248 4 322336. The hospital dispensary opens Monday–Friday from 08:00 to 16:00, and Saturdays from 08:00 to 12:30.
Optometrists, tel: 248 4 321993 or 321177.

EMERGENCIES
Ambulance, Police, Fire, tel: 999
Ambulance, tel: 151.
Hospital, Mount Fleuri, Mahé, tel: 248 4 388000.

GAY TRAVELLERS
There are no gay clubs in Seychelles, but the Seychellois choose not to betray any homophobia.

HEALTH HAZARDS
Sandflies are a real problem on some beaches, especially on those with seaweed lying heavy on them. They are minute and itch like crazy. **Do not** underestimate them. Use a preventative cream or lotion such as Bushman Ultra (80% Deet). **Slippery surfaces** – marble, granite, even man-made wooden decks in hotels can be deadly after rain. Seychelles has no malaria but does have **dengue**. Air conditioning can lead to colds as you acclimatize. Fans are best for mosquitoes. **Sunburn** can ruin your first few days, so be careful. **Coral scratches** should be treated immediately as they quickly become infected. Wear trainers when walking on exposed reef or in seaweedy or grey sand water, but also watch where you walk. **Sea urchin spines** should be removed if they come out easily, but left if they don't. As with **jellyfish stings** and **stonefish poisoning**, immerse the area in the hottest water you can stand. This will help deactivate the toxin, and then seek medical advice. Under no circumstances pick up large and 100% deadly **cone** shells. The ugly **stonefish** that lurks in sand underwater is highly poisonous but rarely

CONVERSION CHART

From	To	Multiply By
Millimetres	Inches	0.0394
Metres	Yards	1.0936
Metres	Feet	3.281
Kilometres	Miles	0.6214
Square kilometres	Square miles	0.386
Hectares	Acres	2.471
Litres	Pints	1.760
Kilograms	Pounds	2.205
Tonnes	Tons	0.984
To convert Celsius to Fahrenheit: x 9 ÷ 5 + 32		

encountered. **Centipedes** and scorpions are very rare. **AIDS**, as everywhere else in the world, is also found in Seychelles.

SECURITY

Violent crime is rare. Seychelles is a fairly wealthy country. Bag-snatching is almost unheard of. Petty theft occurs on some beaches, now patrolled by police. Lock your car. Many hotels have safes. Resorts on some islands deliberately have no keys to indicate security.

Central Police Station, Victoria, tel: 248 4 288000.

WOMEN TRAVELLERS

Avoid obvious risks like walking about alone at night or swimming alone on deserted beaches. Bus travel is perfectly safe. Topless is fine on the beach.

SMOKING

Only where there is no roof above and no walls around you. Or underwater.

LANGUAGE

Kreol, a language mainly derived from French (but written phonetically and therefore difficult to decipher at first from its French origins), is the main language. But English and French are also official languages. Italian and German are understood by many tour operators and hoteliers. With visitors from the Middle East, South Africa, and Russia, it is hardly surprising that Arabic,

Afrikaans, Malayalam, and even Slovenian are increasingly heard in Seychelles.

SPORTS

The following are all available in Seychelles:

Golf. Reef Golf Club Hotel, tel: 248 4 376251, or Lémuria, Praslin (18-hole, championship) tel: 248 4 281281.

Tennis and Squash. Many of the hotels have courts. Try Plantation Club, Le Méridien Barbarons; also National Sports Council Courts in Mont Fleuri.

Windsurfing. Try Beau Vallon Bay or the lovely Côte d'Or on Praslin.

Riding (on the beach and water only). Le Méridien Barbarons, tel: 248 4 673000; also on La Digue.

Sailing. The Yacht Club in Victoria welcomes temporary members, tel: 248 4 322362. Day sailing around Mahé with lunch on spacious catamarans. Mason's Travel, tel: 248 4 288888.

Diving (and learning to dive). Underwater Centre, Coral Strand Hotel, tel: 248 4 621000. As well as this centre, there are many others.

Deep-sea fishing. Marine Charter, tel: 248 4 322126.

Waterskiing. Various hotels offer waterskiing, as do operators at Beau Vallon Bay and elsewhere.

Surfing. Sometimes the surfing is good at Grand'Anse in Mahé. Not many boards are available in Seychelles.

Paragliding. At Beau Vallon Bay. Beach operators.

Walking. There are a number of marked trails on Mahé and from the Coco de Mer Hotel on Praslin and on La Digue. Leaflets and guides are available.

NIGHTLIFE

Large hotels have dinner dances at weekends featuring Kreol dancing floor shows. Learn the sega. There are several casinos where demure lady croupiers will smilingly relieve you of your holiday savings.

ANOTHER WORLD

Seychelles Tourism Board: tel: 248 4 671300, e-mail: info@seychelles.travel website: www.seychelles.travel/

PUBLIC HOLIDAYS

New Year
1 and 2 January
Good Friday
Easter Sunday
Labour Day
1 May
Liberation Day
5 June
National Reconciliation Day
18 June
Independence Day
29 June
Assumption Day (La Digue Festival)
15 August
All Saints Day
1 November
Feast of the Immaculate Conception
8 December
Christmas Day
25 December

INDEX